Thrifty
GARDENING

Also by Marjorie Harris

MARJORIE HARRIS

Thrifty

GARDENING

FROM THE GROUND UP

ANANSI

This edition published in 2012 by
House of Anansi Press Inc.
110 Spadina Avenue, Suite 801
Toronto, ON M5V 2K4
Tel. 416-363-4343
Fax 416-363-1017
www.anansi.ca

Distributed in Canada by	Distributed in the United States by
HarperCollins Canada Ltd.	Publishers Group West
1995 Markham Road	1700 Fourth Street
Scarborough, ON M1B 5M8	Berkeley, CA 94710
Toll-free tel. 1-800-387-0117	Toll-free tel. 1-800-788-3123

House of Anansi Press is committed to protecting our natural environment. As part of our efforts, the interior of this book is printed on paper that contains 100% post-consumer recycled fibres, is acid-free, and is processed chlorine-free.

16 15 14 13 12   1 2 3 4 5

Library and Archives Canada Cataloguing in Publication

Harris, Marjorie
Thrifty gardening : from the ground up / Marjorie Harris.

ISBN 978-0-88784-271-9

1. Gardening. I. Title.

SB453.H38 2012 635 C2011-904018-2

Library of Congress Control Number: 2011929950

Jacket design: Alysia Shewchuk
Text design: Sari Naworynski
Typesetting: Alysia Shewchuk
Interior illustrations: introduction, chapters 1–3, 9, 10, appleuzr/iStockphoto; chapters 4, 5, 7, bubaone/iStockphoto; chapter 6, jameslee1/iStockphoto; chapter 8, browndogstudies/iStockphoto

We acknowledge for their financial support of our publishing program the Canada Council for the Arts, the Ontario Arts Council, and the Government of Canada through the Canada Book Fund.

Printed and bound in Canada

CONTENTS

THRIFTY GARDENING

THE THRIFTY
GARDENER

W hen I first set out to make a garden there was no disparity between my being a gardener and being thrifty. I was as frugal in the garden as anywhere else in my life, so it was a habit right from the beginning. Little did I know that I would become an obsessed gardener with profound needs for rare or unusual (*ergo* expensive) plants. It didn't take very many years to get there.

At first, I made a vegetable garden, not to be thrifty but because I wanted my kids to taste vegetables straight from the garden. I was under the illusion that this would encourage them to actually *eat* a vegetable, a notion they disabused me of pretty quickly. But we all had fun planting every year until we were swamped by the brooding shade of a neighbouring weeping willow. I became a perennial shade gardener by default and by then the kids had weaned themselves away from home.

There is something about making a garden that goes way beyond the intense pleasure of the act itself. And when you start to get compliments, you are doomed. You long to become more accomplished, to discover better ways of growing plants, or to make your surroundings even more delicious. Then, the minute you realize you couldn't care less if anyone else likes what you are doing and that you do it for yourself alone, a seismic shift takes place. You've become a crazed gardener and for that there is no cure.

This breed of gardener is a curious mix: A person who will travel miles to get a free plant and then turn around and spend what seems like a fortune on one that is not guaranteed to survive, even with lots of attention. There is no logic here but it's one of those endearing qualities about gardeners.

There are two extremes of the species: Those who say, "I'll spend anything I have to on my garden, damn the expense." And the others who say, "I'll spend as little on the garden as I possibly can and get the most bang for the buck." The thrifty gardener stands right smack in the middle of those two extremes. The thrifty gardener will think of ingenious ways to save money on the garden and then blow the budget buying a plant that is more than likely to die in a year because it is so rare, or is not hardy, or it's so new nobody knows what it will do. The thrifty gardener dreams very large dreams.

Neither extreme, however, precludes making a great garden. Just like oodles of space or deep pockets can't necessarily produce the perfect garden. I've seen plenty of gardens that have had buckets of money thrown at them, and they still look as miserable as their unhappy owners. Gardening has become more expensive and no wonder. The price of fuel has skyrocketed, plants come from greater distances, and the demands we place on nurseries have gone from "get me the new and unusual" to "give me a deal."

Over the decades, we have become much more adventurous gardeners and it's reflected in how many glorious new plants we can find in nurseries each year — and such are the huge temptations flung at the thrifty gardener. I know all this because I've talked to gardeners of all stripes for the past thirty-odd years. I've prowled around their gardens, interviewed them, photographed their favourite plants, written about them, and designed some of their gardens. And I've learned a lot from all three aspects of my life: doing my own gardening; researching and writing about gardens; looking at what other people start with and what they do, and the attitudes they have toward the space they are confronted with.

The big issue is always budget. Most people can't even bear to think about a budget when it comes to the garden. It's the last thing on the list in a renovation, usually long after the money's been gobbled up by expensive doodads in the bathroom.

You may think you have a budget because you've saved up a few hundred or even several thousand dollars. But it isn't a real budget until you've figured out what that money is supposed to buy. If it includes new fences, paths, pergolas, and lighting, you are looking at big bucks. And notice there's no mention of plants there. Rather than have a costly, time-consuming gavotte when you hire a designer or landscaper, it's best to know what you need and then what you want to spend. And it's critical to be realistic about it.

Two principles are a must to create a thrifty garden with style:

1. Know what you want the garden to do for you.
2. Know what you can *realistically* spend on the garden.

These two principles demand a fair amount of self-examination. Though the garden is often at the bottom of the list of what you feel you can afford to spend on your whole property, there is a false economy here. Gardens are too often treated as a bit of frippery rather than the life-saving aesthetic they really are. There is no longer any argument about the fact that gardening will improve your health. It is a creative outlet open to anyone with a trowel. Stick a depressed person in a garden and within a few hours those deep blues will lighten up. A lovingly tended garden can make you a healthier and probably happier person. Apart from anything else, it is a good investment since it will enhance your property's value.

Gardening is, in a funny way, one of the thriftiest of all hobbies because it's easy to do and you don't need a lot of fancy equipment. Relatively speaking, the returns are huge. But to make a new garden, whether you're starting out in a condo or moving from a large to small garden, it's critical to do it properly from the beginning. That is the only way to save a lot of money — to be thrifty — in the long run. The frugal adage, *Buy well, and you buy once*, applies as much to gardening as it does to all other aspects of life. .

We change house a lot in contemporary society. The nature of those moves can be traumatic or they can be a lot of fun. What I want to cover in this book is just how essential gardens are to all aspects of the thrifty life and how, through the garden, we can adapt to, and even enjoy, the massive changes life throws at us. A garden is an extension of your home. It can be another room, or an extension of a room, and it can be an enormous comfort whether you are young or old.

In the following pages, I will present my own ideas about thrifty gardening, as well as those of some of the best and most interesting gardeners I know. We'll share our tips based on years of experience, and pleasure, working the soil.

The intellectual quality of gardening can never be overestimated. This is a pastime that requires a lot of reading and study, as well as physical labour. The paramount aspect of gardening, however, is that it reconnects us with nature, an innate bond that the brilliant American biologist Edward O. Wilson calls *biophilia* — love of nature. (If you want to hit the intellectual side of gardening, you have to read Wilson's work. He will change the way you look at everything around you.)

You don't need a lot to create a garden that will have an impact on everything else in your life, no matter where you live or how old you are. But you do need to make an effort. And being a thrifty gardener means *scaling your dreams to your resources*. It means recognizing precisely what you can do physically and how much you can afford in time and money — and having a glorious time doing it.

CHAPTER 1

BUYING AND RENOVATING
A GARDEN

To my knowledge, few people in the market for a new home look *specifically* for a house that has a lovely garden surrounding it. I know a few garden mavens who have bought a house on a big lot because they had space envy, including one maven on my own street. She'd been looking longingly at a house on a double lot for years and, when it went on the market, she struck a deal as fast as she could. It was the land she lusted after and she's still there decades later.

Most people, however, consider interior needs far more important than their exterior wants. Most of us know how to cook so we look at the kitchen before we take into consideration the surrounding yard. But as Toronto real estate agent Gil Goldstein says, "It's really a combination of the architecture *and* the planting that sells the house. A lot of people are intimidated by gardens because that's the last bit of expertise they'll acquire. I can't tell you how often I've heard, 'How am I going to take care of all of this?' "

There are a lot of things to be wary of when buying a new garden. For instance, in our neighbourhood, a hugely expensive front garden was installed strictly to sell a semi-detached house for over a million dollars. A mishmash of trees (Japanese maples, a honey locust, and a redbud), a huge hydrangea, a large thorny barberry (along a walk), several grasses, and some hostas had been stuffed ineptly into expensive stonework, which the new owners will eventually have to remove because inevitably the plants will die. A simple and elegant design would have been just as good and less work down the road for the new owner. This was not a good investment on anyone's part.

So if you are a buyer with gardening ambitions, avoid a place with this type of expensive hardscaping unless you are madly in love with the design. It's costly to undo, and it's much easier to start out with a *tabula rasa*, a clean slate. Consider it a greater opportunity to be creative.

If you buy a house with a garden, do your best to keep it tidy until you can get around to making it your own. Give yourself a year — at minimum, three seasons — to see what's been planted, what is thriving, and what has to be tossed. Then get cracking on a garden renovation. If you can't do it yourself, hire someone with fresh ideas to come in and make suggestions. You'll probably save money in the long run.

When it comes to drawing up any kind of real estate/renovation budget, the major mistake people make is to leave garden considerations to the very last or, worse, out of the mix altogether. The anthem is: we'll fix up the house and *then* get to the garden. This usually happens during a time of chaos when all the fancy new appliances are in place but the budget's shot. And what's surrounding the house/reno is an unholy mess — hardly a garden, and certainly not soul-enhancing.

When you buy or renovate a house, don't leave the garden planning until last. It's far too depressing to pick your way through junk for months on end. Fixing the garden even in a minor way can lift your spirits and give you hope that it isn't going to be what you suspect: double the time and money before everything is finished. Even the hint of a garden gives a feeling that the whole upside-down mess might end soon. A garden *always* gives a sense of promise and, with most construction or renovations, you need that — and a mass of hope.

Start with a garden budget right off the top. It can be just a tiny percentage of your total budget. If, say, the renovation is $40,000 just set aside $400. I would love to say put aside 10 percent, which would be more realistic. However, let's go with the lowest possible amount and know that it's not much but it will buy a few yards of good soil.

THE THRIFTY GARDENER'S HOUSE-HUNTING TIPS AND TOOLS

The true frugalista will do a lot of research before buying a house, keeping an eye out for what is do-it-yourself and where experts should come in and do the work (and save money). Here are the essential house-hunting tools:

- A trowel for soil check
- Small carpenter's level to check the grade
- A screwdriver to poke holes in very hard ground

You can easily stick these small items in a bag and keep it with you when you go toodling about looking at different properties. Have no shame. You are about to make the biggest investment of your life.

The thrifty gardener will also look carefully at what's surrounding the house, certainly before making a commitment. Here's what to watch out for:

- Puddling water might mean there's a sewer break or a source of underground water (a faulty watering system comes to mind) that will have to be fixed. Find out the source, see if it's affordable to repair the leak, and try to use it as a bargaining tool in your negotiations.
- Be very careful that the land is graded away from the house.

If it slopes toward the house, it can bring damp and moisture into the building itself. This will have to be remedied before you can be confident that the house is high and dry. A home inspector should be able to explain this but a lot of first-time buyers don't pay attention.

◆ If you are looking at a condo, the same principle applies: Make sure the terrace or balcony is graded away from the living area. A lot of construction, even in really expensive buildings, is being done by inexperienced workers. Take your carpenter's level with you and check it out, because a badly draining balcony or terrace can be prohibitively expensive and complicated to mend.

◆ Find out if there are spring floods. You could be on a flood-plain or you might have the neighbours' gardens draining into yours. It will need fixing, preferably not at your own expense.

◆ In a buyer's market, real estate agent Gil Goldstein says you could negotiate a really terrible yard into a lower price.

◆ Be careful of buried oil tanks. A pipe coming up near the house might signal the potentially huge expense of treating this hidden problem.

◆ Check the local laws about fence heights. Disagreements with neighbours over shared elements can be a major source of expense and irritation, so know what you can expect. Can you cope with having neighbours living right on top of you, or will you want more privacy? Can you install a fence or a fast-growing hedge? At what cost?

◆ Have there been other territorial fights between neighbours? If so, over what?

◆ Look at the trees surrounding the lot. Do they overhang in a threatening way? Will it mean getting huge limbs removed before it's safe to work outside? Is this going to be at your expense or your neighbour's?

◆ What's the view like? If you buy in winter, you'll have to imagine how dense the surrounding trees will be. If you buy in summer, will neighbours be able to see into your house during the winter?

◆ If you're looking at a landscaper-designed garden, be sure to dig into the soil (here's where the trowel comes in handy) and see how far down the good stuff really goes. There might only be a few inches of good soil rather than the 18 inches (45 cm) you'll need to grow trees. Go below the mulch that is inevitably dumped on top of the soil simply to make the garden look superficially good.

◆ Find out if there's a swimming pool that has been filled in on the property. Swimming pools are incredibly difficult to remove, and usually the area around the pool is made up of construction debris and any planting has been done between chunks of metal and cement.

◆ Check to see how the trees are placed: If they've been planted too low or too high and are prone to drying out, they could have a very short life.

♦ Poke your trowel or screwdriver in the soil and pull up a small handful. If it's very dense and sticky, it has a lot of clay. If it crumbles easily, it has more sand. Watch out for trees just plunked into heavy clay; the roots won't penetrate beyond the planting hole and the trees cannot possibly thrive.

♦ Lift the edge of any newly laid sod and check what's under there. It's likely to be barren subsoil, which is useless for growing grass, let alone trees and shrubs.

♦ If there's been new stonework installed and you don't feel confident about it, have an expert check it out. The edges should line up perfectly. Nothing should jiggle, and you should be able to sit and walk on the edges of raised beds if they are installed properly. And make sure you respond to the quality of the stone: Cheap stone looks cheap. Stone is such a lively medium, you must like it a lot to live with it for a long time.

♦ Make sure any planting pockets in the stonework are large enough to accommodate the plants; too often, plants are just stuffed in haphazardly.

A common problem connected with townhouse developments is nice-looking raised beds at the back of the property creating a courtyard feel — except nothing will grow. This is what took place: The

THE LITTLE POOL OF HORRORS

Former Governor General of Canada, the Honourable Adrienne Clarkson is a writer and a dedicated gardener. But she was almost stymied at her new home, a quirky Victorian right in the middle of the city.

Buying a home that had been a rooming house for sixty years and has a level parking lot where you intend to put your garden is in itself quite a challenge! We had budgeted a certain amount for the garden, which we thought was fairly generous. But when we started digging up the asphalt, we discovered tiny blue and white tiles, which indicated that there had once been a swimming pool underneath the pavement. At first, we hoped that it might be a hot tub but, alas, it was a pool 12 feet (3.6 m) long by 10 feet (3 m) wide and 8 feet (2.4 m) deep. We started digging and turned up old bicycles, baby carriages, plastic cartons, and brooms. Apparently the owners had given permission to neighbours to throw any junk they wanted into the pool when it was decided to pave it over for a parking lot. No bodies, thank heavens!

It was the little pool of horrors. It took three solid weeks of jackhammering with the help of three men to dig out the swimming pool and then fill it up with rocks and gravel. This work added about 50 percent to the cost of making our garden. There was no question that we had to do it and, in the end, the garden shows no traces of the old pool, except mysteriously a pale blue tile sometimes emerges when we are planting a new shrub.

good soil is at the bottom of the bed and all the trash from excavation is dumped on top of it. The raised beds built around this pile act as convenient and cheap storage, saving the builder big bucks because he doesn't have to dispose of heavy material. The top few inches of soil will be decent with a few plants put into it. But they won't grow once the root systems start developing.

The following are unfortunately the norms in new house construction:

- All the topsoil is carted away to be resold (or, worse, used as clean fill).
- If it's left in place, the soil becomes so compacted by heavy machinery that it dies a certain death and must be removed or restored with a lot of work.
- The soil from the excavation (subsoil mostly cluttered with stones) is piled on good soil. A little bit of new soil is added on top and covered with sod or a mass of ground cover such as periwinkle (*Vinca minor*). Voilà, a garden. It might take hold over the years but that's not guaranteed. Sod will last a couple of years and just fade away.

An ex-swimming pool is a real problem for any thrifty gardener. It's like tentacles reaching out from the past: We once tackled a garden where the swimming pool debris wasn't completely removed — simply shoved to the back of the property and buried in wretchedly hard clay soil. Plants were bunged in on top. The new trees were quite literally swimming in bowls of clay, and the poor owner had no idea why they were so lacklustre when she'd spent so much money buying them. The contractor had spread a thick layer of mulch over the borders but didn't dig out space for the trees to spread their roots. We excavated extensively around the trees and shrubs, creating large swathes of soil, and then did massive amounts of top dressing with duck compost.

Then we took the most invasive plants — in this case every landscaper's fall-back shrub, false spirea (*Sorbaria sorbifolia*), which is way too vigorous for most gardens, so normally I wouldn't even consider it — and planted them on top of the worst of the dumped soil. They actually carried on blooming, proving that most plants have a useful value — somewhere. But do this with caution. We also moved fifteen weigelas that had been boringly massed near the house to the back of the garden, where they made a graceful low hedge with a lovely pink flush.

If you are ever stuck with a bad design and bad solutions, don't feel you can't have a garden. Repurpose what you've got; even overused plants (like that weigela and the false spirea) can be utilized in refreshing new ways.

THE THRIFTY GARDENER'S RENOVATION TIPS

It's not that difficult to organize a future garden if you think about it ahead of the wrecking ball. You've got to make a deal with the contractor that the workers cannot use the entire yard, back and front, as a dumping ground for materials and equipment. They are plant-blind and even if you show them where your plants are growing, it's simply not important enough for that memory to take hold. Give written orders and a planting plan, something concrete.

A good part of the budget in garden renovations is sucked dry by major removals: Wood, chunks of stone and cement, piles of clay from the basement, and junk, junk, junk. By the time we clear out everything and see what's really happening, the poor client is usually terrified by the estimates for prep and we haven't even started talking plants. Our little company has heard the litany time and again: The contractor says, "We'll do the cleanup, and my nephew loves gardening so we can do a garden as well."

Do not fall for this. Most building contractors know zip about gardens and their nephews know even less about soil and plants. It might look good for the short haul but it's not going to last. Get the contractor to do the cleanup only. If you can, hire them to excavate areas where new soil is needed and make sure it's part of the construction budget as well. This way you won't be on the hook for huge amounts of money without getting the real job done of bringing soil back to life.

Don't put in a garden unless you are prepared to spend time and money on the soil. I keep emphasizing this point because it is the hallmark of the frugal garden.

Here's what every new buyer can do to save a lot of money in the long run when they decide to renovate:

◆ Demand that all the topsoil be saved and stored elsewhere on site. Add as much compost or manure to the berm (the

GARDEN OASIS

Avid gardener Gemma Norton spent two decades transforming expanses of lawn into a richly layered garden, and found the journey was as memorable as the final result. Here's her story.

Grass, grass, and more grass — that was the garden when we purchased our home near Edwards Gardens in Toronto. But I saw POTENTIAL.

A friend came over and gasped, "Oxygen!" at the sight of a mature stand of twelve spruces, a towering cedar hedge, and parkland behind us.

Over the years we put in a dramatic 250-square-foot (23-square-metre) berm in front of the ranch bungalow: Blue carpet junipers, willowleaf cotoneasters, and dozens of stonecrops provided the bones. A Bobcat, guided by a superb designer, carefully placed 4.5 tons (4 metric tons) of cubic limestone in the space and soon an array of ground covers clambered blissfully over the rocks.

I attended a workshop on water gardens where the lecturer spoke extensively about ponds, ponds, ponds. When I asked about a stream, she snorted, "Oh that's impossible!"

The following summer, we put in a babbling brook 50 feet (15 m) long with another 50 feet (15 m) of dry streambed. A recycling pump in the central pond sent 3,000 gallons (11,350 litres) an hour gushing along the watercourse. The sound of the water blocked out all traffic noise. Music to our ears.

Moss-covered rocks, Japanese maples, ligularia, Siberian iris, corkscrew hazel, and sweet woodruff enhanced the banks. A stone inukshuk welcomed visitors to the shade garden underneath the spruces. In the snow I dressed him in a red toque and red mittens.

Twenty years of passion was poured into that garden. . . . A move to Victoria, B.C., prompted a fast sell of the property. The new owners told us, "The garden sold the house."

They were ecstatic. Three months later, the house was on the market again. This growing family had no time for gardening. Was the house bulldozed? I don't know. Here in the gardening paradise of Victoria, my happy memories live on.

mound the soil will make) as soon as possible. It will work its way into the soil and make it more friable (easy to work) when you get around to using it.

- Rescue as many plants as possible. If you can't do it yourself, hire someone who knows how. And that would be somebody who knows plants intimately. It's easy enough to rip a tree out of the garden and take it somewhere else. Doing it properly is a whole other level of expertise. Contractors usually don't have this skill.

- Protect the soil around trees: It's the law in some cities to have protective barriers built around mature trees. Strangely, once a tree barrier has been erected, all thoughts about the tree vanish. It's safe, right? Wrong. You must add lots of compost and manure to the soil inside the barrier, and make sure it's watered regularly.

- Keep all the plants surrounding the perimeter of the property in good condition (composted, watered, protected from machinery) because you'll need them for coverage and privacy.

My last (and hopefully final) renovation was adding a garden dining-room to the back of the house — a structure that took the place of our deck. I'd used the same construction crew for an earlier renovation so they already knew that I'm a difficult perfectionist. They also know my garden is my job (office, library, reference room) so the contractor agreed to put up snow fences a sensible number of feet from the house, and make it a rule that the lads couldn't move beyond the fence. Workers will do what you ask of them, but if you don't give clear instructions, they are going to toss out stuff the easiest way possible. I heard some muttering and grumbling, but at the end of the project, it was possible to see how quickly the garden could be revived. It's a really efficient solution for the gardener, though not necessarily great for storage of wood or large pieces of equipment. So work out a plan for how equipment and materials can be stored out ahead of time and provide a list of rules. Post this paper somewhere everyone can see it. Make lots of copies.

Buying and then renovating a garden is often fraught with problems. Never listen to anyone who says they can create a no-work garden. Nothing is worthwhile unless it takes an effort. And the very first step to a glorious outdoor oasis is by good design.

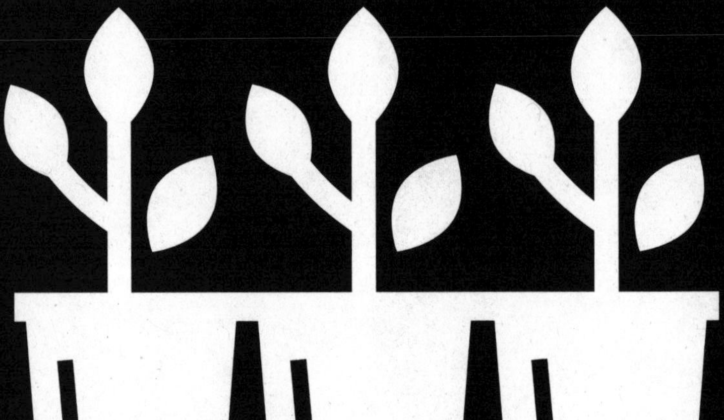

CHAPTER 2

DESIGNING
A GARDEN

A few months ago, I was sitting outside a friend's place having a glass of wine when I looked across the street to my house and viewed my front garden from a perspective I'd never seen before. It was a mess. I couldn't believe it could look that bad. The following day I tore the whole thing out and, within a few days, I had a fantastic new garden.

I know lots of people who have boring gardens, but I make my living at this stuff: Writing about and fixing up gardens. How could I have let my own turn into such a mess? How could I have put up with the inarticulate moosh my garden had turned into? I've found we become so very used to what's around us, that we become garden blind. Yet once you make the move toward a new garden it becomes thrilling. Getting started, however, can be difficult.

To begin a garden should never be complicated but, inevitably, it is. We garden because we seek solace, not to acquire another pain in the neck. But you can make a new garden fairly easily and become a thrifty gardener in the process. The first major move is never to jump into a garden project without thinking it through very carefully.

CREATING A GARDEN BUDGET

If there is one thing you have to face realistically, it's the budget. Nasty as it is to think about money, it comes first in a garden. There's no point in having ideas that will cost $10,000 to accomplish when you have only a few hundred in your pocket.

So having an idea of what you need from the garden goes hand in hand with a decent budget right off the top. Most of us don't relish the thought of figuring out how much a garden will cost, partly because of aesthetics and partly because we hate thinking about money, period.

No garden is going to be dead cheap; it's just not possible. But if you have an annual budget, you can relax and know just how far you can go each year.

Believe me, good design embraces good financial planning, and a really good design will break down the work into components — projects to do each season or year by year as more money comes along. Have what you can afford at the ready, whether it's $150 or $1,500 or

$15,000, and stick to it. Then break down that amount into sections:

- Soil preparation: 25 percent
- Hardscaping (raised beds, fences, screens, patio): 50 percent
- Plants: 25 percent

This is one way of allotting money. Of course, the hardscaping is going to be the biggest expense, but it can be planned into the future. You first need to invest properly in getting the soil ready for plants. And unless you have a huge budget, these three elements are going to be happening one at a time.

In the garden design game, there is a gambit wherein the client thinks, "If I say how much money I've got, the designer/landscaper/gardening professional will spend it all; if I find out how much it will cost, I might save something." Forget about it. Everybody wants a deal and in no other business like this one does the old adage hold truer: *You get what you pay for.* Be chintzy on how you prepare the garden, go for the lowest bidders on structures, buy plants only when you get a deal, and you'll end up with something mediocre and unsatisfying.

Be reasonable. No garden is going to be dead cheap. But where it gets really expensive is making mistakes in the first place.

CHOOSING A LANDSCAPE ARCHITECT, DESIGNER, GARDENER

Sometimes the best and thriftiest solution is to hire a professional.

This is especially true if you are up against a wall for time or simply don't know where to turn next. A good pro will ask the right questions, give you sound advice, and provide you with a garden that will make you happy for a long time. Here's how the profession roughly breaks down:

- **A landscape architect** is responsible for the whole job, including creating a design for all the hardscaping (the gazebos, waterfalls, paths, new garage). He or she will also include site management (making sure people show up and do what they said they'll do for the price quoted). Landscape architects are highly educated and have a ton of knowledge about hardscaping (the stonework, the French drain, and the structures), but don't necessarily know a lot about plants beyond a basic simple repertoire of iron-clad plants used in all their gardens.

- **A garden/landscape designer** will probably have some training but not the years and years of education it takes to become a professional landscape architect. Such designers will have experience in creating gardens, doing the hardscape, and planting. Many know a lot about both construction and plants, but they are rare. Here's where you need to look at past work and see if it is what appeals to you.

- **A gardener** is someone who does the maintenance — all the chores such as planting, weeding, and watering — and who should be well acquainted with how plants grow. A lot of gardeners are really knowledgeable and others wouldn't know the difference between a perennial and a weed. It's best to find out just how good they are. And if you do want help, you don't have to put up with leaf-blowers and all the noisy machinery of urban horticulture. You can demand a no-machine schedule. If they don't want to do it, find someone else.

Whatever help you are looking for, it's thrifty to be cautious. You don't want to become a laboratory or an experimental station for someone's ego, nor do you want to pay for something that's just a copy of everybody else's garden. Here are a few red flags to watch out for:

- **Be wary of "statements."** Anyone who wants to put in dozens of the same plants (shrubs, perennials) to "make a statement" may be lazy rather than creative. Too many of the same plants will go beyond being a drift and just look cluttered. If a disease hits one, it will hit them all. I've seen twenty-one variegated dogwoods squeezed into a small front garden. In a year or so, it looked liked like a mess because each one gets huge. Yes, it did look fantastic in winter with all those red twigs, but the same effect could have been achieved with far fewer plants.
- **Be careful of trends.** Planting in blocks is very trendy right now and doesn't really require a lot of imagination. Ten each of six kinds of plants does not make a great design. The

designer should have a reason for suggesting each plant that goes into the garden: How it relates to the others, the similarity of their light requirements, and whether the colours and textures harmonize or contrast.

- **Beware of plant ignorance.** If a designer suggests shoving sun-loving plants in a shady spot, for instance, reconsider that person's work. It pays to do a bit of plant research yourself to make sure you end up with harmonious combinations of healthy plants, not warring factions of faltering ones.
- **Be very careful if it seems too cheap.** As I've said before: You really do get what you pay for in the gardening biz.

I have one surefire way of figuring out if landscapers know their onions or not and that's to see if they think peat moss is a fertilizer. If they do, *do not hire them.* Peat moss is a sterile medium and, if it isn't applied properly, it will suck the life out of the soil. Many long-time landscapers know very little about the actual plants, but they've been doing the lawn mowing and leaf blowing for so long that gardening is now their profession. But it's like any other work: How good is it? How devoted are the workers? And how knowledgeable are they about plants?

You can hire companies with good software and they can do endless little drawings for you very inexpensively. I've heard of pros dumping eighty designs on a hapless client. This doesn't mean they are doing anything at all creative.

At a recent horticultural trade show, one of the great plant grow-ers of our time, Dan Heims, was there to tell us what new plants would be in nurseries and how to care for them. Next door, there was a sales pitch for expensive gardening-design software. You don't have to guess which place had more people in attendance. Having a cute little draw-ing isn't necessarily going to produce a good design.

So do a check on the certification (many areas have very high stan-dards of certification, others very little) of a landscaper or designer. Or look at other work they've done. This is a time-consuming process, but it could be invaluable. And, of course, you have every right to ask a designer/landscaper to give you an estimate of the job, but don't waste anyone's time. Give a ballpark of what you're willing to spend. Good design does not come cheap.

The Arborist

I highly recommend hiring a certified arborist to evaluate the trees in your garden. It may seem like a lot of money upfront, but hiring a professional arborist will save you big bucks over the long haul, which is the essence of frugality. Amortize the cost over three years, which is how long it will be before you need another serious pruning. It *is* like getting a really good haircut and then you can put on your very best duds to get the complete stylish look. But until the tree doctor comes, you can do the following if you've got some strength and the right tools:

A GARDEN COMMUNITY

Savvy plantswoman Valerie Murray has inspired me ever since I did a story on her magnificent garden in Victoria, B.C., many years ago. She is always just slightly ahead of the gardening crowd. Over the years, I've watched as she has simplified her garden, a process spurred by the long hours she now works as both a volunteer and administrator in a public garden. As she explains, "I didn't want to come home after a long day and have my garden beat me up."

Her life changed when she became director of another distinguished public garden, and changed again when she left. "I found out that your heart doesn't break when you leave a garden you love. Once you live without it for some time, you realize you've survived. You are always only the steward of a garden for a little while."

This is such a smart attitude — one we'll all have to learn eventually. Here are some of her thrifty garden tips:

♦ The best plants always come from garden groups. The tradition in gardening was to exchange plants over the garden fence. Well, that may not happen anymore but the garden clubs and horticultural societies are a great substitute. Quite often members haven't the time or find it hard to fuss around putting plants into containers but will be very happy if you volunteer to come and dig up a plant, any plant.

♦ You'll learn more about plants, what to expect from them, and how to look after them from garden groups than any other way. Our garden club gives you a list of chores you should be doing every month. It's very local and very good.

♦ Make the decision to learn what not to waste money on. If you have to do more repetition in your garden, that's just fine. Think of it as imposed design — if you can't afford to buy a lot of the very new stuff, just keep on repeating, "We need more *Hakonechloa* here. We'll keep that look going."

Valerie's concept of garden design imposed by a plant budget is very smart. But you want to be sure that the plants you are going to repeat are really good ones and worthy of the attention repetition will bring them. Too often a contemporary garden is nothing *but* repetition. You don't want a garden filled with endless drifts of, say, astilbes (a plant that grows in the shade but will take sun and seems to have no enemies). Believe me, you'll get sick of them. Garden writer Felder Rushing says, "There are no clichéd plants, just clichéd gardeners." He is so right. There is no need to drive a plant into clichédom by overuse. Every plant has a personality and should be treated individually and helped to fit in with all the other characters around.

- ◆ Remove slummy-looking trees and shrubs. There are indeed weed trees, and one of the worst is the tree of heaven (*Ailanthus altissima*). It suckers, spreads its seeds widely, and will make a very tall forest within a very few years. These opportunists elbow out the native plants and usually anything seriously worthwhile. They grab the sunlight and shade out plants that don't like to be shaded. Whack them right back to the ground.
- ◆ Dig out stumps or cut the stump so it's level with the ground and cover it with manure or compost. It will take decades for the roots to die completely but this is a simple and very cheap

solution. Otherwise, you're in for the expense of a mechanical stump-grinder or a person to come and hack it all up and try to dig it out. For this you need a very strong chap with a mattock, which is like a pickaxe but smaller with sharp edges. It's a good tool to get out all the tough root systems.

- Alternatively, keep a stump, or any part of a tree, or any beautifully formed dead shrub as a place to put containers or act as a trellis for vines.

It may not sound frugal to have someone else cut the grass, water the plants, or cut down the trees. But I'm being realistic. People need gardens, but gardens need work and not everyone has the time to do it. It's smart and frugal to be cognizant about what you want and what you will actually use your garden for. Will it be for entertaining? A respite? Or a way to enhance the architecture of the house? Good gardeners think a lot about these subjects.

Keep in mind that you are looking for a design that will be handsome in all four seasons, which means making the right choices about plants. Think foliage before pretty colours in bloom. Think about a mix of evergreens (winter), grasses (movement all year round), and foliage colour. You want a design that will keep your eye moving through the landscape with the use of colour or repetition, strong forms (paths, the shapes of beds), and sound (a babbling fountain or a small pond). The secrets of a garden are revealed subtly by a good design, never all at once.

HOW TO DESIGN A GARDEN

Many people have a real problem even thinking about garden design. You *make* a garden, don't you? Well, yes, you do, and very often it's one plant at a time. But that, alas, doesn't always lead to a pleasing garden. The design is where thrifty gardening comes into play, on the ground or on high. If you have a vision of what your garden will become (in your head, on paper, with a designer), you will have a very good idea of where you are heading and what kind of style the garden will take on, and therefore you are less likely to make dopey errors. The great bonus will be that you'll have eliminated spending money on items you can't afford, or that won't fit into your space and will eventually have to be tossed.

Knowing where you are heading is as crucial to gardening as it is to driving. If you haven't a clue as to where you are going — and in this case it means having an overall vision of what the garden should look like, and a scheme on how to get there — you'll never reach your destination, which is to be happy with your garden.

A design must be somewhere in your head. And you should accumulate a lot of information right from the start. Plunking a lot of what are increasingly expensive plants in the ground willy-nilly does not produce a graceful garden. You don't have to learn masses of difficult design concepts, but it's nice to feel comfortable with some of them and not to be baffled if you do end up hiring an expert to give you some help. Here are three major concepts to consider:

1. **Style:** Do you see your garden as a riot of colour? A fairly mini-malist place with very few plants and lots of grass? Or massed planters with one colour dominating all others? Whether it's on the ground or on a balcony, know what it is that pleases you by looking at other people's gardens — not necessarily to mimic them, but to figure out the essence of your own pleasure.

2. **Form:** What sort of shape will the garden take? Lots of boxy borders? Borders with wavy effects? Raised beds? One style of container or an eclectic mix?

3. **Content:** Here's the nitty-gritty on the kinds of plants you like and how they relate to each other. When you choose, go for the big stuff first, the verticals of the design (trees and shrubs), followed by the eye-level layer and then the little stuff (ground covers and vines). Always look at the foliage so you have a good selection of types (fine/broad/spiky/ferny) and choose them so you'll have some visual interest in every season.

There are many other design terms you can get yourself snarled up in and beat yourself over the head for not understanding. But the most important step in good garden design is to put your wants on paper: write it, draw it, get someone else to draw it — in other words, *articulate your garden*.

Climate Zones from the Ground Up

Most North American gardeners have a vague idea of what climate zone they live in. This is a way of tying together areas that have the same lowest mean temperature/highest mean temperature. It gives you an idea of how many frost-free days you have.

If you look at plant tags from the U.S., and you live in Canada, add a zone. And, of course, if you are looking at Canadian plants and books and you live in the U.S., deduct a zone: Zone 6 in Canada is the American equivalent of Zone 5.

The same principles apply to ground level and balcony gardens. The higher up you go, the lower the zone will be. With balconies, you can count on it being very cold above the ninth floor and you'd be safe choosing plants from Zones 3 and 4. Though you have to take into account sun, shade, and wind conditions the higher up you are. These are all vague measurements and back up what I've said before: All gardening is an experiment. You learn by doing in this game.

In addition, when designing your garden you'll have to take into consideration if you are on a high table of land, or a hill, or many feet above sea level.

And then there is something called a "microclimate." This is usually a small area in the garden that is slightly warmer or colder than the rest of the garden. Every garden has dozens of microclimates. For instance, the most protected, sunniest spot might be Zone 7 and a hilly, cold, very exposed area might be Zone 5. So you have to experiment constantly, testing the zones and trying out new plants in different areas of your garden.

Plant Placement and Scale

A small urban garden holds many pleasures because it is often the only connection with nature available in our crowded cities. But it can still be daunting to the gardener because the scale is difficult. A huge mass of space, as in a country garden, can be intimidating because you want to fill it up and usually in a hurry. It's often more difficult to design a good small space than a large one. One error in judgment about scale, a loopy way of putting in plants, or faulty planting techniques can't be hidden in a small garden.

Plant Placement

The perfect placement of even one shrub or tree can define a garden. It can stand alone as a specimen to be admired from all sides, or it can set the tone for how to carry on with the rest of your planting. Move it around, backward, forward, left to right and again until you have it in a spot that looks great no matter where you see it from. It sounds fiddly and it is, but a major plant out of whack will eventually drive you crazy. Even a few inches can make a huge difference, which is why it's worth-while to take plenty of time. This is fussy-creative not fussy-irritating. It's like placing a sculpture in a gallery, museum, or your living room and it's just as important. Here are a few useful tips on plant placement:

- Place trees, shrubs, and plants to create the most amount of shade at the height of the noonday sun, without blocking any delicious view.

- Keep in mind just how tall and, especially, how wide your plants are going to get. The sizes on the plant tags are guesstimates; the final size will depend on how good your soil is, the amount of light, and the severity of winters. But follow all the rules in this book, and your plants will probably be bigger than the tags say.

- Move awkward plants around on an old wooden toboggan or a dolly-like contraption — a plant holder with wheels or a gizmo called a plant caddy — or use a PotLifter (it has straps that cinch around a container and two handles so two people can share a heavy load). Any of these inexpensive items will make hauling around a big tree or shrub very easy, and you can experiment with placement in your garden or on your balcony.

- Look at the tree or shrub from every angle and decide which is the "face" or best side of the plant. This is very much like knowing your own best angle for the camera. One side will be more gorgeous than any other. Turn the face to where you'll be looking at it most often.

Garden design can be as easy or as difficult as your imagination can make it. But going the simplest route possible is the best. Get to know your site intimately and it will signal what it needs or can hold. Then prep thoroughly. Never skip this step. Then start working on bringing your vision into reality.

GARDENING IN COTTAGE COUNTRY

Barry Porteous is one of those happy gardeners who made his decision to move to cottage country many years ago. This is his story.

In 1969 I purchased an acre of land with lake frontage in the Muskoka region of Southern Ontario. At first, the site looked impossible. Glaciers had removed most of the topsoil; summers were mild and wet; the rain and snow were highly acidic; winters were harsh with lows of -35° to -40°C; groundhogs and rabbits ate the vegetables; and chipmunks dug up the bulbs. Now, some forty years later, I have discovered that an amazing number of plants from all over the world will not only grow but also thrive here.

Being Scottish, I had always wanted to grow heathers (*Erica* and *Calluna* spp.), which succeeded so well I wrote about my experience but some disputed my results. What people fail to consider is the amount of snow, a wonderful insulator, we get thanks to our proximity to Georgian Bay. Decades later, these same heathers continue to flourish and are used as ground covers, thus eliminating the need for weeding.

In the early 1970s, I joined the Canadian Rhododendron Society and began planting rhodos and azaleas (*Rhododendron* spp.). While these loved the damp, acidic conditions, very few were hardy and most only bloomed if they were covered with snow. As always, there were exceptions, the most successful being the Northern Lights series, hybridized in Minnesota. The original plants — 'Rosy Lights', 'White Lights', and 'Pink Lights' — have now formed bushes 8.3 feet (2.5 m) high and 6.6 feet (2 m) wide with most of the other members of the series doing well.

Some plants from the southern hemisphere do well: red hot pokers (*Kniphofia*) from South Africa thrive, with the best hybrids being 'Star of Baden-Baden' and 'Alcazar'.

Peruvian lilies (*Alstroemeria*) from South America have proven to be long lived and bloom prolifically. In addition, they have the ability to bury themselves, by as much as 30 inches (75 cm) into the ground, thus avoiding the worst of winter temperatures. Plants from New Zealand have generally been neither easy to find nor hardy, with one exception: mirrorplant (*Coprosma petriei*), a shrubby ground-hugger with translucent, pale blue berries.

My favourite European genus is the *Daphne*. Though very hard to come by at one time, many daphne species can now be purchased locally. Some form prostrate mats while others can be up to 5 feet (1.5 m) in height, with the vast majority being intensely fragrant.

Closer to home, buckwheats (*Eriogonum*), penstemons (*Penstemon*), and bitterroots (*Lewisia*) from Western North America all do well if given a sunny spot with excellent drainage.

Scale

As with art and architecture, so it is with gardening — scale is incredibly important. You get one part of a design that's out of whack with the size of your garden and it will bother you until you change it. To read books or look at magazines is all very well. But since a garden is a four-dimensional work of art (there is time to consider as well), it's really best to look at what other people have done, from botanical gardens to garden tours to the neighbours — it's all fodder for your aesthetics.

Gardeners are instinctively nosy, so stroll the neighbourhood and pretty soon you'll know what's good and what just doesn't work. The trick is to figure out why. That takes what I've long called "creative staring." You spend enough time looking at something, and it will come together in your head. "This garden is all wrong because . . ."

- ♦ The scale of the structures is wrong for the size of the house.
- ♦ The colours of the foliage don't go with the colour of the brick or stonework.
- ♦ The plants don't fit well with the chainlink fence.

You can go on and on, but be sure to make a list of what you think is wrong and another of what's right. Once you've spent some time looking at gardens, your instincts will kick in, telling you what works and what doesn't.

Where most people fall down is in creating different layers of a garden. They are used to the upper-level verticals (trees) and the lower-level horizontals (perennials and annuals). But it's that magic space in the middle (eye level) that's going to make a huge difference. This is where you look for small trees, large shrubs, and tall perennials to fill in that mid-area. So while it's important to work out a planting plan that is utterly satisfying, placement is what makes a design work or not.

DESIGNING A BALCONY GARDEN

When I lived in apartments many decades ago, it never occurred to me to make a garden. Oh yes, I aired out the house plants for the summer, but that was about it. I was saving my gardening efforts for the time when we could afford a house — a real home. That's where a garden would be suitable. At the time there was a "poor you" attitude toward the apartment dweller, reflecting a sense of impermanence about apartment living, that it was a mere stop-off point until something better came along. And it was symbolized by the lack of décor on the buildings.

A trip to Europe in the 1980s changed that view. Every balcony was flooded with scarlet geraniums and cobalt spikes of lavender growing in and around the humblest places. They all screamed, "I'm home!" Such outrageous exterior decoration was barely seen on North American apartment buildings.

But over the decades tiny changes became evident — little gardens appeared, not many, but enough so they stood out like jewels on dreary building faces. I've been watching for the revolution ever since. And it is here. It's no longer just young people waiting to buy a house who occupy apartments; it's older people retiring to condos and well-heeled hipsters who are committed to the high-rise life as a pleasant alternative to carrying a gigantic mortgage and the responsibility of managing a lot of space.

A devoted apartment or condo dweller views the balcony with a completely different set of eyes from someone using it as a temporary perch. The latter will have a "Why bother?" attitude. A permanent resident sees the balcony not only as a challenge to make gorgeous, but also as a way to grab more living space. Going from a garden on the ground into a condo or apartment, however, is something no one can quite prepare you for. It's certainly up there with the seismic shifts life can dish out.

A balcony may seem like nothing but howling winds and uncertain light — quite a change after a lifetime of rooting around in the glories of soil and appreciating different kinds of sun and shade. A whole world of difference — almost like learning a new language. A garden on high, of course, is just as much of a garden as one on the ground and has its own ecological profile. You aren't just putting something outside that will be visually interesting; you are making a difference to the atmosphere all around you. Chances are you will attract birds, butterflies, and insects in need of succour. In addition, you'll be helping to clean up some of the surrounding polluted air with your plants.

And never give up: I know a woman who has a west-facing ninth-floor balcony on which she found she couldn't grow anything (she wasn't there often enough to keep the plants watered, and that brutal late-day sun was unbearable for even the toughest plants). So she replaced her lovely boxwoods and evergreens with plastic forms of the same. It suited her and it worked for the birds too. Before she knew it, they were nesting and providing her with as much amusement and comfort as they had in and among the real stuff. They were looking for shelter and in the city any protected place can be just that — a refuge from the elements.

To create a balcony garden, start with a plan, a design, a sense of the future of the space, and, as always, be realistic about your budget. All principles of garden design apply to balconies or terraces or roofs.

You need to know about your site conditions (wind, sun, rain), and you need to have an idea of what the balcony's function will be (entertainment area, growing space, private retreat). And be aware of scale so you can make the best possible use of limited space.

If possible, think about the balcony garden before you plunk down the money to buy a condo or sign the lease on an apartment. See if it's going to serve you well. If you are a keen gardener stuck with a Juliet balcony, this will not make you happy. And don't opt for something that's too narrow or too tiny. You will want to sit outside in comfort, and you will want to surround yourself with the plants that will give you both protection and joy.

Make sure you know what the building's regulations are (there will be a gazillion of them). For example:

- Find out if there are rules for balcony gardening. For instance, some buildings won't allow you to have anything overhanging the railing (this is normal). You'll often find there's a handy list of dos and don'ts available from the manager.
- Make sure there's an outdoor spigot for watering, as well as an electrical outlet (you never know what it will be useful for beyond lighting).
- Find out how to get plants and soil up to your place and, most important, where you're going to store everything.

Essentially, you can't just barrel ahead thinking, "It's my property, I can do what I want with it." You have a canvas, but you have to make your work of art fit inside the limits you've been presented with and have accepted.

Scale for Balcony Gardeners

As with in-ground gardens, scale is an essential consideration. Have a look from every vantage point — from where you regularly sit or gaze, inside and out. What have you got? Do you have some glorious piece of architecture as your view, or a dreadful factory? It's unwise to exclude either extreme from your design. You can frame the lovely (the cathedral) or block out the ghastly (a factory) with plants or screens. The focal points viewed from inside are important. When you sit in the living room, what should be emphasized on the balcony?

Here's how to save money on the whole design process:

◆ Mock up a plant (or structure) in cardboard and prop it up outside. Then go back inside, sit down, and absorb what effect that height and volume is going to have visually for you. Does it work as a focal point/frame/screen? You can do this sort of maquette with all the plants, but it's most sensible just to do it with all the major structures or really big plants. The scale is what will please, and must be bang-on at such close proximity.

♦ Then start measuring. Break up the space guided by your most pressing needs: How much space should be given over to plants? How much to seating? What should be left untouched? Measure the inside space, then measure all the pieces you need to put on the balcony and see what's reasonable for seating, for containers, or for an eating area. If sitting and eating on the balcony are more important than masses of plants, place your furniture or the suitable maquette in position and see what's left over. Don't overstuff a small area or it will be smothering instead of charming.

Go simple, be elegant. Restricted space is a factor that often exasperates people. But scale works here just the way it does anywhere else. You don't want ditzy containers making your eye dart all over the place, or furniture and plants that are too big or too small. Attitude counts for much in the garden and if you think of your space as a great area in which to have the most graceful plants that are pleasing in all four seasons, you'll have won part of the battle. Now that's something truly exciting to aim for.

Light

The rigidity of working with a small, unalterable space can be exhilarating: You know the exact parameters you'll be working with and there will be few surprises. You can figure out what the wind's like and how the light conditions change over the course of the day. These considerations are critical to a balcony's ability to sustain plants. It's easy enough to figure out what direction you are facing, but how many hours of sunlight actually fall on your balcony in midsummer? In spring? This will dictate whether you can have herbs and vegetables (they need six hours), hostas (only a few hours), or shade-loving annuals (indirect light).

There are aspects of every exposure to take into consideration:

- ◆ North facing: Light might bounce off the surrounding buildings, illuminating even a seemingly dark space.
- ◆ South facing: The higher up you are, the more intense that searing sun will be and the more difficult it will be to grow plants. Think xeriscape (drought-resistant) plants and alpines.
- ◆ West facing: The hottest sun of the day. But if you are nestled among trees on a lower floor, you'll have the joy of sunsets and none of the intemperate hours of blinding sun. From the ninth floor and up, you'll have to take this heat into consideration as you plan your garden.
- ◆ East facing: The easiest place to have a balcony garden. You get morning light and avoid the most severe heat of the day. And there will be enough light bounce to make a successful garden.

Balcony gardens are exciting places to be because they are always with you. You see them all day, every day, so the smallest details become critical, but you can have so much fun working on them to create a fourth wall of the apartment.

The Prevailing Wind

The major problem confronting the balcony gardener is the wind. It is going to end up being your enemy (and in some cases can be close to insurmountable). Therefore, it's wise to find out where the prevailing winds swoop in from and see if you're in full blast or alee. Many plants can't cope with non-stop wind so there's no point trying to grow those particular ones. I've watched people plant Japanese maples on exposed balconies only to have them die within a season. The point of thrifty gardening is not to waste any money.

It's impossible to halt the action of the wind, but you can break its killing force by growing evergreens and plants with dense foliage. If you can attach a screen along a wind-ridden edge of a planter box on the interior side of the balcony, you've already got a small, protected spot for a vine and it might stand a chance of survival. You can huddle your most delicate plants in front of other tough plants and you've got two things going: 1) Layering, which is visually pleasing and therefore an important over-all design element; and 2) A spot for either contrasts or harmonies in the plants you choose.

AN OASIS IN THE SKY

Carol Cowan is a hortbuddy and a committed high-rise dweller who loves her building with the same intensity as anyone on the ground. I love driving by Carol's building because you look up and there it is: A beacon of plants. But even better is sitting with a glass of wine on a summer evening enjoying her plants. And for good reason — she really does have an oasis in the sky. Here's what she does.

I have a terrific ninth-floor, west-facing balcony. It's wonderfully long — 28 feet (8.4 m), yet miserably narrow at just over 4 feet (1.2 m). With the exception of two comfy chairs, a little table and an old Persian carpet, which defines the central seating area, the balcony is planted from one end to the other.

Decorative annuals inter-planted with parsley, rosemary, and lavender fill two window boxes and a variety of containers, all of which can be seen from the living and dining rooms, and then there's "the back forty," as I like to call it, where I grow herbs, tomatoes, cayenne peppers, all-season strawberries, and even zucchini and peaches-and-cream corn. To date, the annuals and veggies have been uber-thrifty acquisitions, as I have been trialling them for a supermarket and garden-centre chain.

However, the best thing I ever did — before the condo outlawed such things, although mine are now "grandfathered," whew! — was to firmly affix (with sturdy, plastic zip ties) to the balcony railings, three sets of wrought-iron garden gates, 12 feet (3.6 m) wide in total, to form a trellis on which I grow a variety of vines. As a result, I have the pleasure of eye-level greenery as well as a bit of protection from the blazing afternoon summer sunshine.

Being thrifty in the world of high-rise gardening is all about containers big enough in which to over-winter perennials. I've lucked out with a couple of really cheap (under $30 each) yet pretty black plastic pedestal urns that are about 18 inches (45 cm) deep. Placed on either side of the trellis, they're planted with Virginia creeper (*Parthenocissus quinquefolia*), a great, inexpensive vine that's hardy to Zone 3. They have now come back for four years, and each summer cover more and more of the trellis.

In the middle of the trellis, my yearly splurge is to grow mandevilla (*Mandevilla*) for its lovely pink trumpet-shaped flowers and passion flower vine (*Passiflora incarnata*), with its amazing other-worldly blossoms. All three vines are sun-loving and can withstand the ever-blowing prevailing winds.

Another inspired choice that I'll certainly repeat was the purchase of a $15 Kentia palm (*Howea forsteriana*). Placed in front of the trellis so it gets dappled sunlight that prevents leaf burn, it's obviously very happy as it's popped out a new frond every three weeks of the summer. The leaf- and flower-covered trellis and the bushy palm, now 5 feet (1.5 m) tall, are among the highlights of my tropical urban oasis in the sky.

ORGANIZING STORAGE SPACE ON THE GROUND OR ON HIGH

You may be surprised to see organizing equipment in the same chapter as designing a garden, but they go hand in hand. You have to think about storage at the same time you are designing, no matter what kind of a garden you have. Equipment piled up in a corner is not pretty and that's one of the points of making a good garden. When it comes to organizing, all the principles of thriftiness come into play.

Take a long hard look at how you store your garden equipment and essentials. It's pointless keeping unused tools: Get rid of them and if you can't do it on your own then get help. The thrifty way to go is to hire a professional. The idea of hiring an organizer to come and fix a messy basement is not unusual, but why not apply the same principle to the balcony or garden shed? I'm here to testify that it's a thrifty action at any time of life but it's especially useful when you want to downsize.

I chose Kate Seaver, who not only knows how to garden but is also an expert clutterbuster. It turned out to be money well-spent. Since the garden shed was built in the 1980s it's become a magnet for every single thing I've bought since then. The shed seems indestructible, but it's the repository for anything I don't want to see lying around in the garden. When I opened the door, I could see Fibber McGee–type chaos, but in a flash Kate saw it organized. And I was gratified to know that she'd seen worse. By the time we finished this project, I knew where everything was and how to make that kind of order spread outward into the garden.

Some facts to face up to: 80 percent of all new gardeners do not have a plan for where they'll do their work or store their garden tools. It's an afterthought. Everyone needs a bench, a potting shed, a place for everything from the garden — no matter what size the garden is. So here are some tips:

- First of all, decide where you are going to do various tasks and how big a space you need. If you're going to use the kitchen table for record-keeping, seed-sorting, plant research, garden design and such, organize with that in mind. Think about a work area for things like potting up, dividing plants, taking cuttings, growing seeds, and cleaning or repairing tools.

- If you haven't used something for two years, consider tossing it, donating it, or selling it at a garage sale. You can always get rid of things for a few dollars.

- It could be worthwhile storing the best-quality items that might not be in style right now. Things come back into fashion in gardening pretty quickly.

Effective organizing means knowing what's central to your style of gardening, determining what tools and work space you really need, and making what you'll use easy and simple to get at.

Balcony Storage

It's best to think of this up front. Where do you put even the modest amount of equipment you'll need? Some buildings have good storage spaces in the basement, but no one wants to be tearing up and down just to get what's needed on a daily basis. Check out the elevators and the space allotment before you invest in any equipment or plants.

Consider how much you can realistically store on the balcony itself. Do it with style: A bench with a lid is always an excellent solution. If you look at designs online, they are not the most graceful *objets*. Time to use the imagination and look around for some thrifty alternatives:

- Footstools with a lid. If the surfaces aren't weatherproof, you'll need a winter cover. Many very up-to-date outdoor furniture lines have great low tables-cum-footstools with a lid. Make sure the interior is lined properly to protect the tools inside.
- Kid's toy boxes are well-built and practically indestructible. Look in toy shops for kits or for old ones in junque and second-hand stores.
- Blanket boxes come in all sizes and, if you can find one that's in good shape, use it.

Add cushions on top of any of these choices, and there'll be extra seating as well as a neat place to keep soil, mulch, your tools, and even a coiled hose.

Collector, gardener, and dear friend Ted Johnston adds the following:

- Old wooden toolboxes can be painted and are cheap. They make terrific storage boxes or you can use them as seats or cover them up with pots.
- Cheap wicker trunks, painted with outdoor paint can look terrific. Things might get wet but it doesn't really matter for most garden equipment.

If you have a terrace or garden on a rooftop, try large plastic bins and cover them in very stylish plastic tablecloths. They can be used as side tables during a dinner party. And they cost about $10.

Once you've got a sense of the style you want for your backyard or balcony garden, and you've worked on a design and how you will organize your garden, you can be confident that you've made some good choices, you haven't wasted any money, and you know where you are heading. Gardening is confusing only if you are uninformed about what you have. Knowing what you can do and having a budget means you can sort out what you can afford year by year. Now onward to shopping for plants and equipment — the heart and soul of thrifty gardening.

CHAPTER 3

SHOPPING FOR
THE GARDEN

Once you've decided on how you'll approach the garden design, it's time to tackle getting the essentials. I love garden shopping — way more fun than shopping for clothes. Over the years, I've bought an amazing number of tools and gizmos but have also gone through many different stages trying to scale back my wants to line up with my needs. I have a large enough garden that it requires three outlets for watering, *ergo* three hoses; and I like to use top-of-the-line equipment.

In my garden design company we have three to five people working on any job. They each have their own tools because they are craftspeople and prefer to use their own equipment rather than my stuff. And it was a lesson to me to learn what they considered essential compared with all those things I have cached away at home.

Monique Dobson is a gardener, and I always call her Dr. Monique because she can make any sick plant better. She always lugs about what she calls the Pail of Life — one pail full of implements that are vital to her work (many, many different cutting instruments: she is an amazing pruner). We all tend to have something like this on the go. We're a pretty motley lot of men and women but we don't have one piece of electric equipment among us. So I set out to watch what I actually put in the pail and figured out what my most essential stripped-back list of tools are.

THE THRIFTY GARDENING TOOL BASICS

Before you make your own list, commit yourself to never being cheap about the basics. You may think something's expensive, but amortize the cost over years of use and instantly it's a bargain. My favourite example is a trowel I bought in England for $75 in 1989, an outrageous amount of money for a garden tool at the time and probably still is if you factor in inflation. It's gorgeous and has never lost its marvellous feel in my hand. It's always at my side and is as important to me as it is to my garden.

Cheap stuff tends to fall apart fairly quickly plus there is that iconic factor: They become junk rather than a symbol of your love of the garden. And naturally, you tend to take better care of good equipment than anything that's disposable or cheap. Be sure to set aside one day a year (usually at the end of the season) to clean, oil, and otherwise fix tools. Store them properly. This way your equipment will last forever and you've established a pleasant ritual. A beautifully crafted tool is even more enjoyable when it's buffed up — especially the older ones.

One exception to the list below: Efficient secateurs of any size can be expensive so I like to have one really good pair I use all the time, plus several less expensive ones for persnickety little jobs (and to replace those that walk off by themselves). Secateurs tend to get put down on the ground as you wander around, drawn by the needs of another plant somewhere else. I've found them in the weirdest places: Stuck in containers, under a shrub, in the composter (I've also found my sunglasses in there). To repeat: Gardening can be one giant distraction, and it's just not possible to be focused all the time.

Here's the most basic equipment you'll need for any size garden:

- ◆ **Trowels:** A trowel will handle all the small planting and dividing jobs. A good one will have a deep dish made of stainless steel with an ash handle. It should have a nice weight and a good sense of balance. There are two kinds to get: One with a wide, long dish; and the other with a long, narrow dish. The latter is a transplanting trowel and is really nifty for popping in bulbs or small plants. Scale the size of the trowel to the size of the job: a big one can make fairly substantial holes; a little one can snuggle in between plants.

- **Secateurs:** Hand-held tools with a scissor-like action, these are the pruning essentials. You can cut off thin branches or deadhead a flower with them. You need at least one good strong pair that will cut up to a three-quarter-inch (2 cm) branch, plus a smaller pair to keep on your person at all times. There are many famous brands, offering both types of secateurs: Anvil for tough stuff, and bypass for everything else.

- **Tiny deadheading scissors:** These are the little snippers with a sharp little tip that are perfect for precise delicate work such as deadheading (cutting off spent blooms). They are cheap and you can find them in Chinatown and more recently in nurseries.

- **Planting spade:** This is a smallish workhorse of a tool. It has a square shape and won't heft anything heavy, but it is ideal when you want to make sharp edges for your borders or paths. It's useful for lots of little jobs and easy to store.

- **Shovel:** A long-handled shovel will make short work of digging substantial holes and humping shrubs around.

- **Water meter:** This instrument will tell you when your plants need to be watered. I had no idea this was a necessity until I got one and now feel it's a garden essential. You can stick them in containers (in and out of the house), near shrubs and trees to get a sense of just how deep the water is going. Always keep the tips clean.

- **Small rake:** A child's toy rake is handy for whipping out debris stuck between plants. I like a little wooden one I found many years ago, but any kind of a small rake will do.
- **Leaf rakes:** There are dozens of ergonomic versions around. Buy one if you have a lot of leaves to pick up. Otherwise just let fallen leaves lie.
- **Hoses:** Get a good one, not a cheap one. There are kink-free hoses now, and I liked one so much I traded in all my old ones (some with forty years of service) and have found these new ones to be easy to handle and really efficient.
- **Broom:** A small straw broom keeps a space tidy.
- **Bag Balm:** We all have nuts and bolts that we can't do without. Mine is Bag Balm, the stuff farmers use to keep their cows' teats soft. It's cheap and it's almost pure lanolin. Slather it on hands and feet and occasionally dab it around those little lines around the eyes. Don't go to bed without giving it a whirl. And don't put your feet on the sheets — you'll never get the stain out.

You don't need a lot of equipment to make a good garden. You do need fortitude, determination, and vision. And, please, lots of patience. As my friend Dugald Cameron says, "Impatient gardeners tend to spend more money."

GREAT GARDENERS MAKE ESSENTIAL ADDITIONS

Uli Havermann is one of the finest gardeners I've ever met. She buys garden essentials as deliberately as she does stuff for her well-equipped kitchen. "I have watched, with sympathy, as neighbours try to prune roses with scissors or cut down branches with large unwieldy saws." Here's what Uli would add to my basic list:

♦ A trenching shovel for digging deep holes in tight spaces
♦ A kneeling pad
♦ A box cutter for opening bags
♦ A flat-edged steel rake for levelling soil
♦ A hose reel that can be moved about the garden at will (she has a huge number of plants in containers throughout her garden)
♦ Gardening shoes and boots at each entrance of the house
♦ A large container of pumice soap, the kind mechanics use — available at the hardware store

"It is an absolute must to clean sap off your hands or any major dirt and grit," Uli says. "I have received the bar form of the pumice 'gardener's soap' as a gift, and it is lovely to use."

GARDENING TOOL ESSENTIALS OFF THE GROUND

A balcony or rooftop terrace requires so little equipment even a haute frugalista can afford to buy the best. Stick to the basics, while keeping in mind the ever-present need for space to store same.

- **A trake:** A combination trowel-and-rake — one half looks like a trowel and the other half a small rake. It's useful performing the jobs of both bits of equipment without taking up much space.
- **Small secateurs** or a pair of **Japanese scissors:** For neat deadheading.
- **Spray bottle:** To keep bad bugs at bay.
- **Plastic bags:** For storing, carrying, or recycling old soil or tools.
- **One good trowel:** A good trowel with a narrow dish for transplanting plants or tucking mulch into a small space, or one with a wider dish for digging holes.
- **Hose:** The kind that's like an old curly telephone line is a fine idea if you can store it in a container. Don't invest in one of these until you check out the connection with your taps. It's wasted money if it doesn't work. There are excellent watering systems that combine the curly or coil-up hose, the wand, and an adapter for most taps. This saves both space and money.
- **Watering wand:** You attach this long-handled spout to your hose to make watering on high so easy. The best one has a tip that you can stick right into the plant and lets water flush through softly with good hand control for the pressure.
- **A well-balanced watering can:** It's best to get a watering can you can pick up with one hand when it's full. I happen to have a large Hawes watering can that's done well for about thirty-five years — a worthy investment.

- **A water monitor:** This instrument is to check the moisture in the soil. Clean off the tips each time you use it for a more accurate gauge.

You don't have to spend a lot of money buying equipment for the balcony garden. Just make sure each element is the best and most efficient one for the dollar you spend and that there's a good place to store things.

GOING TO THE NURSERY

When I first started shopping for plants, or for that matter anything at all for the garden, I was riddled with guilt. In those days (forty years ago), plants, at least to my mind, were things you got from other people or found abandoned and in need of rescuing. High-end gardening was not the style as it is these days.

I would never haggle at a garden centre unless I were spending huge amounts of money and it would be along the line of, "If I buy three flats of a plant, can you give me a bit of a discount?" Most nurseries have so many deals, percent-off days, clubs to join with added premiums, that there's *always* a deal. These businesses work on very small margins and I want all my favourite places to stay in business. Those margins are only going to get tighter as the cost of fuel continues to rocket. People will think twice about driving 30 miles just to get a special plant unless there are a lot of other desirable things on offer as well.

I still get a flood of pleasure when I walk into a well-appointed garden centre or a little back-of-beyond surprise of a nursery and I always have the same delighted reaction: "I want everything here." Delight and dismay of course go hand in hand when it comes to shopping for plants. It's one of the most glorious experiences of spring: Walking into a freshly tarted-up nursery jammed with new plants, cash or credit card in hand. This is the best of times and it can also be the devil's playground for the unwary gardener — everything is alluring. You *need* whatever your eye falls on. This is the ultimate thrifty gardener seduction. Resist. And give yourself lots of time to ruminate over your choices while at the nursery. Slow shopping is thrifty shopping. The more you rush, the more you demand things be done in a hurry, the more often it leads to bad decisions. Buy well and you buy once.

Here are some guidelines for going to the nursery:

- Take a list, stick to it. Do not look to the left or the right of what you've come to buy. That's the ideal situation. But we usually need help here because the desire to acquire overtakes you the minute those alpha waves start kicking in.
- When you are looking at the plants you'll buy, make sure there are no weeds in the pots. This is one of the main methods weeds employ to get around. Clean them out yourself if you have to, but don't bring them home. You can bet there will be seeds lurking in the pots themselves so be very cautious and pick through the soil when you get home. This is why shopping quickly is not going to be frugal.

- When buying any plant, make sure you read the tag: What is its ultimate size? How much sun does it need? How much water? Can you supply the space, conditions, and care this plant requires?
- Don't be hustled by a sales gimmick — *"We are selling off cedars today for $9.99"* — unless you really need what's on sale.
- If you do buy a sale item, be it equipment or a plant, make sure it's not damaged or in bad condition.

Plant shopping is exhilarating and such fun that you have to keep firm control of an over-lustful eye. Plants massed in displays are going to look fantastic. Try to be a cautious shopper not an over-excited one.

Here's what plantaholic hortbuddy and garden writer Karen York and others advise when shopping for the garden:

- Shop with frugal friends. Studies show that friends (and even friends of friends) influence everything from how much you weigh to how much you smoke. And at least some unpublished preliminary research shows that friends can influence how you spend as well. Next time you're planning a big-ticket purchase, bring a frugal pal shopping with you.
- Check your emotions. Research from British and American psychologists has found that we're willing to spend more money when emotions run rampant. In fact, in one famous study from Carnegie Mellon, participants who'd been shown a tearjerker about a dying parent were willing to fork over almost

four times more for a bottle of water, compared to people who'd been shown a documentary about the Great Barrier Reef. Save shopping for when you're in a mellow mood.

And here are some more thrifty tips:

- Put all your purchases in a cart, and shift them about until they look good. Anything that looks out of place should be removed immediately.
- It's better to buy less and come back for more on future trips. Trying to stuff everything into your garden at the same time can lead to some confusing combinations and move you away from your overall design. Also, if you're not sure of a plant's performance, buy just one, try it for a year, and only get more if it does well.
- Try using each trip to the nursery to buy a specific category: Shrubs and trees could be one; perennials another; and last, but certainly not least, annuals.
- Wait until containers go on sale at big box stores and super-markets at the end of June before indulging in new purchases. Thrifty gardening is about desire deferred.
- High-end stores will put containers on sale in August or at the end of the season. If items do go on sale, make sure they aren't brutally chipped or marred in some way. They still won't be cheap so you need to have them in good condition.

Arranging and rearranging your plants both in your head and when you are at the nursery is a good way to spend time. Each plant should relate to the one next to it in some graceful way, and they will look even better in the ground.

HOW TO BUY PLANTS

Buying a plant is just as persnickety as buying a new pair of shoes. They have to be a perfect fit and complement what you already have. But they should also lead you forward to other plants with a different texture, scent, or colour in the foliage and the blooms.

Buying Perennials and Annuals

Always look for a nicely shaped plant. It's tempting to buy one that's in bloom, but the best plant is one that has bulk and a good root system — not a showy display of blossoms. Make sure the soil isn't clotted with weeds (leave them behind at the nursery).

Here are some tips on shopping for annuals and perennials from Tom Thomson, one of the most highly respected horticulturalists in Canada, and Dugald Cameron, proprietor of one of the best catalogues published today (www.gardenimport.com) and a self-confessed mad keen shopper:

♦ When buying perennials, think foliage, foliage, foliage. A long bloom time in a perennial means about six weeks. Foliage is for three seasons.

- Whatever your budget, don't buy one of this and one of that (unless it's a perennial you want to test out). With annuals, go for flats of 15 of the same thing and plant them in groups. Flats usually have 15 to 18 small plants in each, so make it five each of three kinds and people will think that you know what you're doing.

- Don't pay top dollar for the latest trendy hosta. The old varieties are cheaper and have a proven track record for wonderful foliage.

- The idea of buying all of your plants over the May 24 weekend ("The garden's done; let's go to the cottage") is madness. Good nurseries have lots of new plants coming in throughout the summer.

- Don't buy from a nursery where a) They don't know what your plant is; and b) They may not be able to identify the source of a problem or what to do about it if it's been hit by a disease. Lumberyards, big box stores, and supermarkets can't afford to keep experts on staff.

- When you find a plant that's terribly pot-bound (overgrown, dried-out roots) give haggling a whirl. Never hurts to try. But not under other circumstances.

- Shop in July when nurseries are trying to move stock.

- Go on garden tours in July when you'll really see what the plants look like. Everyone has a garden tour in June, but July, August, September, October, and November are the great months to look at gardens.

♦ Be very careful of any plant that might have even a molecule of bindweed, goutweed, or horsetail in the soil.

The ideal plant, says Dugald, has many seasons of interest, is hardy and offers abundant fragrant flowers, nice foliage in spring, summer, and fall, and delicious fruit as well. Try to get as many of these factors in one plant as possible.

Purchasing a Tree

A tree will be one of the major purchases you'll make for the garden. No tree is cheap, though, and some can be wildly expensive — I'm talking thousands of dollars. Size counts here: the bigger it is, the more expensive it will be, and the more likely it will need special equipment to transport home.

Always buy a small tree and let it grow into its new location. It will end up being much healthier, better adapted to its space, and you'll know how big you want it to grow. This is not a process that can be put into overdrive. I've seen people waste humongous amounts of money on buying gigantic trees because they want an instant effect. Such a tree can take ages to get established and may or may not flourish. A smaller one, well cared for, is a better investment.

Small trees usually come in big plastic three-gallon pots so you aren't disturbing the roots in a catastrophic way when you pull it out of the bucket. Somewhat larger specimens with rootballs wrapped in burlap (called balled-and-burlapped trees, and often listed as B&B) are a bit trickier. Arborist Derek Welsh says you don't have to do anything about that burlap *if* you buy from a really good grower. Trust them and know that their trees are guaranteed. But be aware that not all growers, nurseries, and landscapers guarantee plants.

When you bring a balled-and-burlapped tree home, untie that knot at the base of the trunk, and cut away at least half of the burlap, leaving the material on the bottom. This process allows for minimal disturbance to the root system, but it will give you a good enough look at the roots to see if they are girdled (wrapped about each other). If the roots are girdled, tease them out so they are lying flat.

A tree is for the long haul, so consider its size at maturity (will it still fit into the garden?). Buying a tree is a thrilling business. Imagine walking through a forest of trees and having to choose just one for your preference; well, going through a nursery is like that. Everything looks fabulous. Be sure to view a tree on all sides to make sure it looks perfect and don't rush the process.

Buying Plants from Catalogues

Catalogues expand your plant possibilities enormously — you can buy all sorts of seeds, bulbs, herbs, perennials, and woody plants from their alluring pages. As in all other aspects of gardening, you have to learn the code. When buying from a catalogue, you must know that "plug" means a very tiny, very young plant that might not come into bloom for a couple of years, let alone survive. "Bare root" means the plant is sent with no soil on the roots; it usually comes wrapped in wet newspaper (many roses are shipped this way). "Open-pollinated" refers to seeds that have been naturally pollinated in the field, rather than hybridized. Some abbreviations to know include:

- ♦ **HA** means hardy annual. This is a seed you can grow outside and scatter in situ.
- ♦ **HHA** means half hardy annual. You'll have to start this seed inside the house, and then plant it outside.
- ♦ **HP** means hardy perennial. You should know whether this perennial will grow well in your area.
- ♦ **HHP** means half hardy perennial. It's a perennial that will do well in warmer climates but will probably be an annual in cold areas.

Keep in mind catalogues are a form of garden porn, meant to lure you into buying these gorgeous plants. They will not look like that. Bare root plants shipped in a dormant (leafless) state arrive looking like dead sticks and you must be prepared to plant them the minute they are delivered. Small leafy plants can arrive miserably wilted; take them out of their boxes, water them gently, and set them in a warm, shady spot to recover. The thrifty gardener will know the right date to plant in the garden in spring or fall (check out your local weather site). Here are a few tips:

- Have a budget in mind before you even open a catalogue. You can rack up huge bills if you aren't careful. Stick everything you like on a list and then cut it in half.
- Figure out how much space you have to start seeds indoors, then revise the list again. Don't take on too many plants when you are starting out or you will be overburdened and probably fail.
- Bulbs can be a good deal purchased in bulk, but beware of small, scrawny bulbs; bigger, more luscious is always better. Many catalogues offer special prices on multiple quantities of plants; it's tempting but watch you don't overbuy.

There are great catalogue companies in every region of North America. But it's important to buy as locally as you can so you're more likely to have plants and seeds that have adapted to your own climate.

Seed Exchanges and Garden Co-ops

No one can fail to marvel at seeds, those magic little packages with a personal DNA that has evolved over the centuries. Seed exchanges are wonderful ways to get seeds, talk to other gardeners, and get a lot of information for free. Seeds of Diversity is an umbrella organization that is dedicated to saving heritage seeds (native plants as well as those that are not cultivated varieties) and have what's called Seedy Saturdays all over North America. People converge in one place to exchange seed packets and listen to speakers. It's an occasion not to be missed.

Bev Wagar, who runs a busy Seedy Saturday program in Port Burwell, Ontario, recommends that the frugal gardener be a co-operative gardener:

♦ Save on bulk mulch or compost delivery charges — order a full truck (5 yards or more) and split it with your neighbour. The driver can dump half in your yard and half next door.

♦ Arrange a seed-order co-op. I'll post the seeds I'm ordering from an online retailer and ask if anyone would like to split the packet with me, so we each pay half or even one-third the cost. Shipping charges are split equally as well. I add a bit for my postage expense, since I have to divide and re-mail the seeds, but the savings are worth it. People who don't want to share my order can order and pay for a full packet but save on the shipping.

♦ Organize a bulb co-op, doing a similar group purchase from a retailer and dividing the orders.

Catalogues and seed exchanges are a great way to further your horticultural education. No matter what you pick up, you'll be learning something fascinating about plants. Now that we have the Internet, there's always a chance as well of meeting like-minded people. But there's no substitute for seeing other gardeners in person, and there are many ways to do that.

THE YARD SALE

The yard sale is the best exercise ever invented for a frugal gardener on the prowl for garden décor or just looking to get rid of stuff. It's always amazing what people will throw out. One of my favourite reclamations is a little kid's fold-up table, which I haul out when I want to repot plants or use as a tray for the barbecue.

Scour every sale you see, always give a glance at what's tossed out on garbage day, and deign to snoop around recycling bins. Who knows what treasures you might find that, with a little elbow grease, could work in the garden. People don't throw out secateurs, but they will get rid of old shovels (nice plant prop), rusty wheelbarrows (good planter), and assorted stuff from the fireplace (fantastic bits and pieces for decorating a fence). This is the place where you can spot items that other people aren't clever enough to hang on to and reuse:

- ♦ **Containers:** Be imaginative about what makes a good container. An old iron pot always looks attractive — though you will have trouble if you can't make a drainage hole. If it's impossible to drill a hole, use it as a *jardinière* — i.e., set a potted plant inside it on a bed of pebbles. Wooden baskets, unusual plastic containers (make sure they haven't had toxic chemicals stored in them), and the boxes trees are delivered in can be hugely useful, especially if you have a balcony garden. Chipped enamel and other vessels can make quite lovely little plant holders. Watering cans make really wonderful decorative elements, painted or not, and the really old ones have some value in the collectible market. Even shattered terracotta can be used as drainage material.

- **Brick containers:** Make your own containers from bricks. Place six bricks in a closed circle. On the next layer, place each brick over the juncture of two bricks, and in the next layer use the same arrangement as the bottom layer. You can make it as high as you wish, though three to five layers usually works well. The container will hold soil and water, or you can hide a plastic pot or bag inside. Think of making an arrangement of two or three of these containers as a focal point. You can dismantle them for winter and keep the bricks in a dry place.
- **Vases:** People abandon vases all the time, so take another look at them with an eye for smashing them up for tiles or for using them in the garden as a design element resting on the ground.
- **Busted-up pottery:** Pop pieces of pottery in the ground near particularly difficult plants as an *aide memoire* that these babies need special attention.
- **Sprinklers:** Before buying an expensive sprinkler, see if you can find one that someone else has decided to do without. Sprinklers baffle most people, but if you are clever, you can probably find one that works.
- **Books:** Some people think garden books date, but I see them as social history and never let an old one go if I can help it.

It's amazing to see what we did in the 1930s, '40s, and '50s. Though we were putting nicotine on the very plants we were going to eat, we were also much more like organic growers before World War II than we have been until recently.

- **Garden magazines:** Yes, you can find good stuff in them but I tend to donate my own sets to botanical libraries (where you can get a tax deduction for donations of books and magazines — talk to your local horticultural library). I hate ripping them apart but if you can bear doing that, make files and keep similar information together. The wonderful thing about magazines, especially from the twentieth-century, is that the photography is gorgeous and we'll never see anything like that again. They are lovely things to muse over during the winter or in the bathtub (where no e-book rests easily).

- **Wood:** Anything made of wood can probably be recycled into something useful in the garden, from a compost screen (old orange boxes) to a bench to hide in a secret part of the garden. Old boards can be used to make a plant stand — prop one between a couple of old ice cream chairs and you've got a French Country look.

- **Check out anything that's galvanized:** It gives a very *moderne* look to any garden. Tubs without the bottoms make excellent raised beds.

- **Bedsteads:** Turned on its side with shelving found in the garbage makes a bedstead a fashionable rusty plant holder.

THE ULTIMO CAST-OFFS

Uli Havermann, who is an experienced scavenger, always scans the garbage even when driving.

I've picked up terracotta pots, galvanized buckets, antique ladders, wooden plant stands, an old watering can, a vintage concrete birdbath, and an antique cast-iron chair with a broken leg that I've propped up with cobblestone.

Our best find was a set of Muskoka furniture — two chairs, a bench, and a small round table. My husband, Paul Zammit, and I were driving home one night and spotted the set on the side of the road. We were close to home but not in a big enough car, so I got out and sat in the chair (squatter's rights) and Paul went home to get the car with the roof rack. Though it took a couple of trips, the furniture has been part of our garden for several years and is only now in need of repair.

My best yard sale find is the set of cast-iron, nineteenth-century urns bought on my way to work one weekend. I saw a garage sale sign and spied some cast-iron pieces in the ditch and a large cardboard sign with the price: $750. I started talking to the owner. He guided me into the garage where there were two complete urns with handles and sculpted bases of herons in reeds, and the support bases that are set into the ground. There was also a complete fountain with two tiers of ornate dishes, a cast-iron support cherub, and the same bases and supports. My heart was pounding — I knew this was going to be a once-in-a-lifetime score for me.

It turned out their daughter was one of my son's closest friends, so her father immediately dropped the price and said he'd hold on to them until I was able to pick them up. And their daughter gave me photographs of herself as a very young girl posing beside them."

Now you might think collecting and placing all of the following would be too much, but Esther Giroux has a fantastic garden. She never over-burdens it with her collectibles but she can cram in a lot of them. She can translate almost anything into a garden artifact. Here are a few of them:

Rusty grilles line the fence; tractor parts (semi-circular disks) are used to prop up plants; old copper tubing from plumbing makes ornamental plant stakes. Old metal picture frames hang on the fence; an old bicycle (bought for $5) is a backdrop for the herb garden; wire dish racks hang on the edge of the deck; a big old galvanized washtub takes the overflow from the rain butt and makes it easy to scoop out water for individual plant watering. But her best find to date is a rusty old bedstead used as a support for clematis.

And here's one not to bother with: Toilet bowls as cute plant hold-ers. They make me feel very humourless.

SCROUNGING

Never go by an old barn, a junkyard, or a recycling plant without checking its contents. You never know what will surface. One of my best old barn finds was an abandoned iron gate, which has now been on my fence for a couple of decades. I've lifted screens, grilles, and fire irons out of the garbage. Gardener Susan Harriell lives in the country and is constantly on the alert for unusual treasures. Here's her best scrounge of the last decade:

"I managed to get my hands on some local barn beams, which match the benches I made out of the floor beams of a nearby 1840s schoolhouse — the owner was going to bury the lovely beams! I persuaded him to simply put them on his tractor shovel, drive them down the dirt side road, and dump them at my home.

"We set them up on logs where they stayed for a couple of years, while I figured out my design. They eventually became five benches. Recently, I added two arbours at the ends of my hill path — two vertical posts with a crossbeam each. Trumpet vine (*Campsis radicans*) is planted at the base of the sunniest one and the native vine, virgin's bower (*Clematis virginiana*), on the shady one. The floor beams meet the thrifty designation. Total cost $0, but I had to purchase the barn beams and they are expensive.

"Our township has a huge pile of shredded mulch in its work yard from the trees and branches they must trim. I persuaded the staff to let a friend come with his big dump truck to pick up a load for me. I have used it to mulch the native shrubs and trees that the government planted along the front of my property and partway up the side fence lines. Cost: $0, cultivating good relations with the township works staff, and a beer for my friend!"

Never be embarrassed about grabbing stuff from sales, the recycling, or the garbage — not when it comes to gardening. The whole world is out there to be reused, employed in a whole new way. Giving new life to old stuff is what gardeners do best.

CHAPTER 4

THE PLANTS

You can fill a garden with waterfalls and follies, pergolas and obelisks, but plants are what make a garden truly glorious. A garden filled with carefully chosen, well-grown plants will be a delight for many, many years, with or without any other enhancements.

I didn't quite understand the artistry of gardening until I saw a photograph of two plants that looked utterly perfect and radiant together. I realized, "Hey, I can do that." I started moving plants around, making new combinations, getting rid of ones that didn't look right, and bringing in fresh plants all the time. I have what's laughingly known as a dense garden, a garden that's so thick with plants, you feel like you are drowning in foliage. But that's my style and it works for me: But I have to always remember that it's my work as well as my pleasure. My garden is my library and a laboratory where I experiment with new plants all the time so I can write about them.

I like to see plants combined for the texture and shape of their leaves. I have one combination of a Japanese umbrella pine (*Sciadopytis verticillata*) with a silver-leafed hellebore (*Helleborus* 'Silver Lace') and a black mondo grass (*Ophiopogon planiscapus* 'Black Knight'). If I am feeling blue any time of the year, including winter, I just go outside and have a look at them and feel better immediately. There is something about how gracefully they complement each other that is so satisfying. That is my aim in all my combos. But it doesn't always work.

Here are some pitfalls:

- Too many plants of one ilk together: Too many variegations, for instance, can make you dizzy just looking at them. One well-placed variegated plant in every border usually adds some luminosity to a design. But there is no hard-and-fast rule about this. Sometimes having two or three variegations can work well together. You have to train your eye to know when you have a surfeit.
- Overused plants in great big drifts. It gets dull seeing street after street with nothing but big puffy hydrangeas and a couple of grasses as an excuse for a garden.

♦ Foliage and bloom colours that don't work well with their
surroundings — for instance, a certain tone in a Japanese
maple clashing with the bricks of the house. Think through
what a plant will look like in every season.

I have many, many prejudices about plants, but there are really
very few I hate. What's so exciting about this mad delight is that there
are endless varieties of them, infinite colours and tones, extraordinary
secrets. And, of course, plants draw in the insects and birds we need to
keep the ecology of the planet in good shape.

THE PERFECT TREE

I am crazy for trees. In my little garden I have planted dozens of them,
and I'll keep on planting more until I run out of space. A winter death
is an opportunity. My choice for the perfect tree or shrub to function as
a focal point, whether it's in the country or a small urban garden, would
come from the following list. They are frugal plants because they give
value for dollar, have four seasons of interest, and cause few problems:

♦ **Paperbark maple** (*Acer griseum*) has exfoliating cinnamon-
coloured bark. It starts out with delicate pinkish tones and turns
into a lovely, almost luminous green during the summer. It has
a huge rootball so don't stick it casually in any old place — give
it room. There is now a new cultivar called 'Cinnamon Flake',
which is smaller and possibly even more gorgeous.

CHEAP AND COMMON

Michele Landsberg is a wonderful writer, feminist advocate, and a long-time hortbuddy. We nip about buying plants and talking endlessly about gardens. She has her own inimitable style in both gardening and writing. She started gardening like so many of us, without a bit of experience. Here's her story.

Like Keats's "stout Cortez" (a lot like stout Cortez, actually) I stood silent and gazed with "wild surmise," not exactly at the Pacific Ocean but at the wilderness of my backyard. Where a sizeable forest of diseased and repulsive Chinese elms grew, I could envisage a fragrant, flowery garden, spiced with all the perfumes of summer and blushing with gentle colours. But how to achieve this vision in a desperate hurry? It was the first summer of my life that I had time to indulge my daydream of gardening. But it was also, possibly, the last summer of my life, because I was in treatment for breast cancer.

And here's where frugality enters into the picture. Frugality and prudence are not my middle names. It was not for reasons of fiscal restraint that I relied on the kindness of friends: it was lack of time (Hurry! Hurry!) and severe lack of energy to shop. This is how I discovered the delight, the generosity, the beauty, and the pleasure of all those deadly enemies of the true gardener: The Grim Invasives. You know them; every garden magazine sternly counsels against giving them foothold. They came to me unchosen, the gift of friends and strangers who heard of my new mania for gardening and of the new clean slate of my backyard border, where the Chinese elms had been efficiently extirpated.

Invasives are what everyone has enough of that they can give away lots. They came as wilted singletons, stems drooping over dirt-clogged roots; as heavy clods in the bottom of green garbage bags; as dead-looking wisps and suspicious clumps. Most of them had no names attached. I planted them all, not knowing any better; thank heaven, goutweed was not among them or I would have been mightily taken with its variegated leaves.

Here's what I learned: most of those so-called invasives are common as dirt. They reproduce with louche abandon. That's why they're called "invasive," which sounds as hostile as a military incursion, but is actually just . . . fecund.

It's human nature to disdain what is common and easily available, but when I gazed upon the bounty nature had bestowed on me the following year, here's what I saw: Clouds of dame's rocket, strewing their phloxy perfume about; green and crisp ostrich ferns, making a small forest under the old summer lilacs; evening primrose, too yellow but still festive; Shasta daisies glowing; periwinkle spreading a glossy carpet underfoot, where previously there had been only mud, starred with purple-blue flowers all season long; bigroot geranium with its intoxicatingly woodsy scent when crushed, willing to grow wherever I tossed it; dancing cosmos of every colour; gorgeous clouds of pink meadow-sweet from a neighbour's cottage; and coneflower, sturdy and vibrant and a snoozing place for innumerable bees.

Not one of these "invasives" ever gave me a moment's trouble. When they demand-ed too much space, it was easy to whisk them out. (Only crown vetch, actually bought and planted by me in my days of innocence, ever deserved the name of a noxious invasive. It strangled everything in its path).

If you can be content with swooning abundance, and not mind that this flourish-ing florascape is cheap and common, go for the invasives. You can get rid of them later, bit by bit, as the garden you have planned at leisure takes shape. But meanwhile, what lusciousness.

- **Dwarf columnar hornbeam** (*Carpinus betulus* 'Columnaris Nana') is a little beauty and ideal for a small garden as a 7-foot (2.1-m) screening plant. The neat birch-like leaves are gorgeous; the shape, elegant.

- **Tricolour beech** (*Fagus sylvatica* 'Roseomarginata') is one of those beech trees that looks good all year long. The bark is a silvery grey, the leaves a luminous combination of purple with a pink and white border. As far as I can tell, in fifteen years it shows no problems whatsoever. It's a tricky colour so make sure you don't put it up against a clashing brick wall.

- **Fernleaf beech** (*F. s.* 'Asplenifolia') is a magnificent plant. I have it as a standard in my own garden, and it's a bit of work keeping it pruned to the right size but worth every minute. Almost everyone comments on it. It's an ideal screening plant when you need a little privacy. Perfect for a small city garden; and for a huge garden let it grow to its natural 60 feet (18 m).

- **Japanese maples** (*Acer palmatum*) come in so many colours, sizes, and shapes that they are poetic and thrilling. I adore these plants. There are several species I particularly like, *A. shirasawanum* being one and *A. p.* var. *dissectum* another. And there are hundreds of cultivars. Look at any Japanese maple and study it. The trees put up with a lot of abuse, but the most egregious habit is to stick one all by itself in a sward of grass. You might as well put them in green cement. They like lots of company and they don't like the blistering noonday sun.

If you can't grow Japanese maples in the ground, grow them in containers (they are the ultimate bonsai plant). Get a very large pot with good depth and make sure you put it out of the wind; otherwise, you might as well expect it to be an annual, which is hardly frugal. They can get huge so read the tags with care. My temptation is always to get them into the ground quickly. But check the roots. Many Japanese maples grown for a mass market don't have strong root systems. Keep a tree with a scrawny rootball in a container in a nice protected spot and let it grow for as long as possible before leaving it alone in the ground. My favourites:

- *Acer palmatum* 'Tamukeyama' has purple/magenta leaves and a fountain shape.
- *A. p.* 'Villa Taranto' has a vase-like shape and deep green foliage.
- *A. shirasawanum* 'Autumn Moon' and *A. s.* 'Aureum' are the plants I visit several times a day just to see them in different lights. The leaves are palmate (like the palm of the hand), golden, and, in the former case, edged with orange.

Garden writer Karen York suggests starting small when it comes to trees. She says, "Good-size specimens of Japanese maple can require a second mortgage, but many nurseries either do their own propagation or bring in small grafted trees. These can often be had for reasonable prices. An added bonus is that you can start pruning and shaping them nicely from an early age. Similarly, with conifers, look out for collections of small conifers in pots aimed at bonsai or container gardens. Again, they're a bargain price and some are surprisingly fast growers. Use them as miniatures in troughs or containers, then transplant them into the garden once they outgrow the pots. If you have a small garden, trees and conifers started early like this won't overwhelm it any time soon, and you get to enjoy them at all stages of their lives."

Look at the trees that grow well in your region. I'll bet you can find a beauty among them that will give you pleasure for decades. And if it's a native tree, all the better.

Native Trees

Native trees are essential for a solid and handsome permanent structure in any garden, and a little research will reveal which ones are best in your area. They are often underused and therefore more difficult to find. But don't let this discourage you. Also look for the understory plants that will not only look good as companions to these trees but will help build up an ecological relationship with them.

In my area, at the edge of the Carolinian forest in central Canada, the following are wonderful trees:

- **Kentucky coffee tree** (*Gymnocladus dioicus*) has a stick-like form in winter, which is its downfall. But in the summer it's a canopy of almost fernlike complexity. The leaves are gigantic and look almost prehistoric (which they are — this is an ancient species once grazed by mastodons).

- **Sourwood** (*Oxydendron arboreum*) is also called lily-of-the-valley tree (it has a similar scent). Flowering in spring, it struggles away in my garden, but I like to keep it because the leaves are so weird and exotic-looking.

- **Tulip tree** (*Liriodendron tulipifera*) has the most striking tulip-shaped blooms: Pale yellow with green and orange stripes that appear in the tree's twentieth year.

- **Eastern redbud** (*Cercis canadensis*). I had a purple-leafed cultivar called 'Forest Pansy' in my garden for many years, and then one day it split in two. It definitely needs to be situated in a protected spot. And I would choose a multi-stemmed specimen next time.

And no garden should be without evergreens, which offer tremendous value. They add presence, unbeatable texture and forms, and year-round colour (not just green, but also blue, grey, gold, and cream).

Every region across the country has a rich mix of native trees to draw on, including these:

- **Paper birch** (*Betula papyrifera*) and **river birch** (*B. nigra*) are gorgeous trees. The exfoliating bark isn't as white as the European forms but they have the advantage of being able to withstand major diseases and insect borers. In England, gardeners power-wash the birches to make them more dramatic, something I find distasteful in the extreme. We don't use these trees enough because they will eventually succumb to pollution, but they are the most dramatic of all our native trees.

- **Red maple** (*Acer rubrum*): One of the stateliest and most glorious of maples. Don't stick it in front of a red brick house, though, as the leaf colour will clash with the orange of the brick. Keep it as a specimen, which means placing it on its own as a focal point.

- **Sugar maple** (*A. saccharum*): You can actually hear and feel the sap rising in this tree, and you might be able to collect a little to boil down. It's fun to show children how plants live. This is a lovely, very large tree and should not be crowded.

- **Serviceberry** (*Amelanchier* spp.): This plant has many names (shadblow, Juneberry, sarvisberry, saskatoon) depending on the locale. Species range from multi-stemmed to single-trunked tree forms. It is one of my favourite four-season plants: glorious white blooms in spring, edible black berries in summer, incredible autumn leaves, and a lovely striated bark in winter. A must.

- **Western red cedar** (*Thuja plicata*): A magnificent evergreen with a lot of history (this was a mainstay for aboriginal peoples), it sort of looks like a cypress, is aromatic, and grows very tall (up to 230 feet/70 m) so place it with caution.

- **Hemlock** (*Tsuga canadensis*): The shape and smell of hemlock speaks of the ancient forests, and, if you have a big enough property, you can't have a more wonderful plant. It will be a nesting place for lots of birds, but it does get huge and needs lots of water. It's a superb conifer that takes a lot of bullying — you can even prune it down to a hedge.

- **Shagbark hickory** (*Carya ovata*): Attractive to people and birds, this tree has fascinating bark (it breaks off in platelets, lending it a shaggy look, thus the name). You can use them on the barbecue. It has a conical shape and grows about 80 feet (25 m) tall.

- **American hornbeam** (*Carpinus caroliniana*): I like the shape of this eastern forest native. It has a lovely form for the garden and also fabulous autumn colour. It gets to 40 feet (12 m) in height and, amazingly, grows well in shade.

When you choose trees for your garden, think about those native to the region before any others. Buy at least one for a central focus. Then pick local evergreens — three is a good number so you have some winter interest. Add smaller trees so the whole garden balances out with many vertical layers, including eye-level, and finally fill in with the other plants.

PERENNIALS VS. ANNUALS

When I started out, my garden was all annuals — nothing but white blooms so they'd glow at night — then I switched to all perennials. Now

I grow both but lean more heavily on the perennials because that's what I've got and because they give so little trouble.

You can't afford to ignore certain kinds of plants if you want to be a thrifty gardener, and any garden without some annuals is poor indeed. They fill in gaps and bring a brightness and shimmer of blossom that most perennials can't match. And there's a reason for this: Annuals have to bloom and make seed for survival so they must look absolutely ravishing to attract pollinators as quickly as possible. You might say they are the divas of the garden. Then the hybridizers fool around with them, making them even more brazen, fluffy, or colourful. My own taste runs to the simpler, classic forms of annuals, but others love the riotous effects that lab work has provided.

Perennials will return year after year, but they don't give instant results unless you buy (or get from another gardener) mature plants, i.e., about three years old.

The little thing you buy in the nursery is going to take at least two to three years before it really does what it's destined to do. People often expect way too much from perennials when what they really want is a big blowsy flower garden.

When people hire me to do a fix of their gardens and want a riot of colour, I tell them up front: I don't do that sort of thing. I concentrate on foliage, and you can add all the zip and colour yourself with annuals. Then, of course, they discover that the perennials get increasingly lush with each passing year and they have much less room for annuals. And there is less expense involved. Then the whole design process changes once again.

Here's what you look for in perennials and annuals; in fact, in plants in general:

- **Contrast in leaf size, shape, and texture.** When you have a garden filled with plants that have the same leaf size and shape, it is incredibly boring. You want the eye to stop and enjoy a variety of complementary sizes, shapes, and textures.
- **Colour.** Try to pick up colours from one plant that will be echoed by the one you're introducing into the garden. These little moments can make gorgeous garden pictures.

Keep these thoughts in mind when you head for the nursery. Even the thriftiest of gardeners can get boggled in early spring with the bounty at the nurseries. It leaves you weak and panting. "I want, I want . . ." Well, don't cave in. Have a concept, a budget, and a list and stick to it.

Perfect Perennials

Some plants are more perfect than others, and coral bells (*Heuchera* spp.) are among the thriftiest perennial plants you can buy. Dan Heims, the president of Terra Nova Plant Nursery, one of North America's top breeders, made this plant one of his great triumphs. Coral bells are no-fail, put up with the worst abuse and manage to survive. "Use their leaves in bouquets," Dan says. "They will actually root in water and can live for years at room temperature in a vase with good water. I know of no other plant that can do this. With a base of *Heuchera* leaves in a vase, flowers can be cycled in and out. Try *Heuchera* 'Purple Petticoats' with medium green and taller black tulips in a vase. Stunning!"

To that, I would add a combination that will perk up any garden, large or small: Put three *Heuchera* 'Blackout' with three (or any odd number you wish) Japanese forest grasses, *Hakonechloa macra* 'All Gold'. The black and the gold together make magnificent edging, and will fill a container or window box with drama. You can make a dazzling splash with a simple arrangement of only a few plants, which is what it takes to be frugal in your initial choices.

No-fail plants will thrive for decades. You can move them around your garden or leave them alone, but you can't live without them. Here are some of my favourite no-fail (*ergo* thrifty) plants, apart from coral bells:

- **Hellebore** (*Helleborus*). Like most plants, hellebores love a well-drained soil. Add lots of organic matter, and make sure that beds are dug deeply so that their rather large root systems will have lots of room to run. Though these plants will grow in the shade, they will take several hours of sun and, of course, in winter they are exposed to both sun and snow. If they are out of your zone, put them in containers lined with Styrofoam and store the containers so the plants won't get exposed to freeze-thaw cycles.
- **Euphorbia**, also called spurge (*Euphorbia*), is practically unkillable. These plants have a nasty latex sap in their stems, which means deer hate them. Be careful when handling them

because that same lactic acid can cause dermatitis. Many euphorbia species are vigorous, which is garden-speak for they will get huge, and will make a statement. But be aware: Myrtle spurge or donkey tail spurge (*E. myrsinites*) is one gorgeous ground cover but it will beat up anything planted around it and cover a vast area. In a container, however, it will be extremely well-behaved.

♦ **Hosta** (*Hosta*). These are fabulous plants, especially for shady city gardens. But people too often use a bunch of exactly the same variety, or accept random plants from others. Better to save up and buy a mix of them to create a deliberate tap-estry effect. They come in many different sizes, colours, and variegations, making them an enormously satisfying plant to collect.

If you are just starting a garden, get annuals for an instant hit of colour, and mix in a few perennials because these will be your main-stay for many years to come. And no matter what you put in the garden, make sure there's at least one black plant. They go with everything.

10 Thriftiest Perennials for Sun

This group of plants, ideal for scree gardens, rockeries, or troughs, was chosen by Harvey Wrightman, one of the leading growers of alpine plants in North America:

1. **Sandwort** (*Arenaria* 'Wallowa Mountains'). A drought-tolerant, bright green mat, not too competitive.

2. **Gypsophila** (*Gypsophila aretioides*). A superb mat with a chocolaty winter colour — very, very hardy.

3. **Speedwell** (*Veronica bombycina*). Silver-grey mats with blue flowers.

4. **Androsace** (*Androsace barbulata*). Tight, low mats that gradually enlarge; fragrant white flowers.

5. **Draba** (*Draba* spp.). Most have yellow flowers; all are attractive to bees.

6. **Moss campion or catchfly** (*Silene acaulis*) has an attractive ferny base with brilliant flowers that range from deep magenta to white. Will cope with light shade.

7. **Gentian** (*Gentiana angustifolia*). Huge, gorgeous blue trumpets from May on; easy to grow and spreads to make a colony. For sun or light shade.

8. **Dwarf daphne** (*Daphne velenovskyi*). One of the best plants for troughs. It has fragrant pink flowers, and will often throw late bloom with no damage in November when temperatures dip to -8 C.

9. **Daphne** (*Daphne arbuscula*). The leaves are a dark "yew" green, and the flowers are fragrant.

10. **Fleabane** (*Erigeron* x 'St. Mary's Peak'). The great Czech plantsman Josef Halda says, "It's the best."

10 Thriftiest Perennials for Shade

1. **Hosta** (*Hosta 'Mt. Kirishima'*). This forms a petite clump of wavy narrow leaves, with exquisite purple flowers.

2. **Lungwort** (*Pulmonaria altaica*). From seed collected by Josef Halda in Siberia, this is a beautiful introduction with large cerulean blue flowers, and leaves that are pure velvet to touch.

3. **Primrose** (*Primula auricula selections*). Primroses comes in so many delightful forms you can collect them all. The colours range from pale yellow to outrageous combinations to black-and-white stripes. Will cope with sun, too.

4. **Allioni's primrose** (*Primula allionii* 'Neon'). This is the best selection there is for reliability and bloom — a dazzling, red-purple.

5. **Pyrenean violet** (*Ramonda myconi*). A hardy, drought- and shade-tolerant gesneriad. It has a rosette at the base, which looks good all the time, and violet-blue blooms.

6. **Resurrection plant** (*Haberlea rhodopensis*). Its common name derives from its habit of almost miraculously reviving from periods of drought with a watering.

7. **Saxifrage** (*Saxifraga paniculata* 'Correvoniana'). White flowers with a distinctive yellow eye.

8. **Stonecrop** (*Sedum spathulifolium* x 'Waight Hybrid'). Silver leaves, dwarf habit, yellow flowers in summer.

9. **Maidenhair spleenwort** (*Asplenium trichomanes*). Ferns grow

magnificently in the shade. This is a special one but you should look at all those that grow in your region. Fantastic plants and some are evergreen.

10. **Shooting star** (*Dodecatheon pulchellum* 'Sooke'). The most spectacular shooting star with large magenta blooms.

Whatever style of garden you want to have, think carefully about the selection of plants. Keep in mind when they will bloom (so there's always something in bloom) and when they will fold up and disappear.

Imperfect Perennials

The following plants will fill up space faster than you can believe possible. Now this may be just what you are looking for: Instant effect. Let any of them go to seed and you'll end up with huge drifts, up to acres of them running into neighbourhood gardens or into an unsuspecting ravine. You will also find all these plants at your local plant sale because everyone else is trying to get rid of them. All these plants are sold in nurseries, usually without a caveat. You've been warned.

- **Garlic chives** (*Allium tuberosum*) is an adorable plant, looks elegant, has stiff scapes and white flowers, but let it go to seed once and you've got hundreds of them. Keep one plant and keep it contained. Move the flowers to a vase.
- **Creeping Jenny** (*Lysimachia nummularia*) is a handsome

little ground cover for a couple of years. Then it spreads madly and you spend the rest of your life pulling it out. It has pretty yellow spring flowers and does nicely when highly controlled in a container with its lovely foliage hanging over the side. Better bet: The golden form, *L. n.* 'Aurea', which spreads much more slowly and looks even more dramatic dripping over the edge of a pot.

♦ **Variegated goutweed** (*Aegopodium podograria*) is the world's worst plant. Grows in deep shade (so it makes a good shade container plant), but it is so rambunctious that it will take over everything, everywhere — sun, shade, wet, dry. It travels by root (making a patch about 80 feet/24 meters in circumference) and seed. If you see anyone planting it, threaten to sue. If you try to pull it out, any scrap of root remaining will make a new mother plant.

♦ **Lily-of-the-valley** (*Convallaria majalis*). Oh, the pretty, white, distinctively scented spring flowers are enticing, but this one will grow in and among and through everything else in your garden.

♦ **Sweet woodruff** (*Galium odoratum*) has glorious white starry blooms and then it will run all over the place. It's easy enough to pull out and that's exactly what you'll be doing for years.

♦ **Northern sea oats** (*Chasmanthium latifolium*). Don't ever hire a landscaper who wants to put this in your garden — it will indicate he knows very little about plants. It's a really good-looking grass, but unless you go out every day and cut off the seedheads, which are its crowning glory and the reason to plant it in the first place, it will seed everywhere.

- **False spirea** (*Sorbaria sorbifolia*) has gorgeous plumes but moves like mad, and should only be planted in cement containers. Still, if you have a huge space you need to keep from eroding, this might be your plant. A great favourite of landscapers, it has become way overused.

If you get stuck with any of these plants, remove them from your garden carefully. The most difficult is goutweed. Snip it back to surface level, then cover it with black plastic held down with bricks for a few hot weeks in spring. Uncover, snip it back, cover it with layers of newspapers and then the black plastic. The trouble really is that it moves into plants and you have the devil of a time trying to untangle it. Keeping at it is the only method of removal.

The Perfect Annuals

Annuals add brilliance to any garden. They will fill spaces left by bulbs fading into yellowing foliage, add luminosity unlike any other plant, and bloom their heads off for months. It's tempting when you are starting a garden to have only plants that give instant satisfaction. But it's not thrifty in the long run. You want a mix. Plant some annuals to please you now but be sure to add perennials, which will get bigger and better as the years go on and you won't have to replace them as you do with annuals.

This is my list of preferred annuals. You'll notice that there is no impatiens on this list. That's not because it's a bad plant — far from it — but it's used so much. It's far more interesting and fun to look a little farther afield. These are a few that give me pleasure year after year. Keep them deadheaded, watered, and tidied up, and they will look fantastic for months.

- **Spurflower** (*Plectranthus* 'Mona Lavender') is the perfect annual, bar none. It will put up with container negligence, in-ground ignorance, and will come indoors to bloom in January. It has silvery green upper leaf, purple lower leaf, and neon indigo-blue flowers, which go on for months. Use it everywhere in the sun or part-shade.
- **Alternanthera** (*Alternanthera* 'Purple Knight') is a wild, upright, gorgeous plant with thick purple leaves. A must-have in at least one container. Works in sun or shade.
- **Canna lily** (*Canna* 'Durban') could be the only spiky plant you need in a container. Its foliage is striped with ice cream colours, which can be picked up in other plants in the design. Needs sun.
- **Coleus** (*Solenostemon scutellarioides* 'Purple Duckfoot'). This stunning coleus — well, any coleus — will catch my attention. Get several to pick up a tone from one and repeat it in another (such as caramel/purple). Take a wee cutting at the end of the season, put it in water, and you've got next year's crop. Needs shade.

CREATIVE GARDENING

Barry Parker is another of those incredibly creative gardeners I've met over my years as a garden journalist. He travels widely, collects seed to get unusual plants, grows hundreds of interesting varieties, and is fascinated by garden design. He manages to combine all his vast interests in one small downtown garden with dozens and dozens of troughs and containers that surround the back of his house.

But in a cruel climate, what does he do in winter with all those containers? He used to gather them up and put them on gravel and then cover them with a cold frame or window frame. Here's what time and experience have dictated:

♦ The plants do fine without any protection and although the cold-frame did give them a good start in the spring, I now find that I have to employ another form of thrift, i.e., a more economical use of energy and less wear and tear on the muscles and skeleton. I shovel snow on the troughs in the early spring as the original fallen snow begins to melt. This keeps them insulated against sudden drops in the temperature, which can easily happen at that time of the year, as well as slowly releasing water onto them as the snow melts.

♦ There are some plants, such as hens-and-chicks (*Sempervivum* spp.), that like to be kept dry over the winter and will tolerate the cold until the weather improves and then they will put on a wonderful show of colour and spectacular geometry. I've wintered them under garden chairs with translucent plastic covers, which create a kind of cold frame (as well as protecting the chair).

♦ I collect all sorts of gravel and rocks, using the gravel to mulch the top of pots. This looks really good with cactus and succulents, and also keeps squirrels from rooting around in the soil.

- If I can't find a rock big enough for a project, I will stick a few together with a glue designed for bonding stone to stone.
- With a little imagination, create a nice container by combining a couple of broken or chipped ceramic pots. Put bowls inside one another, drill holes in each (not just the one on the bottom), and they make great layered containers.
- Plant up troughs with commercial cactus soil, mixing in some Turface (calcined clay) to aerate the soil.

Philippa Campsie and Norman Ball bought a great old house with a derelict garden, which has been transformed over the years. They say that they don't have a planting plan but just keep moving things all season long:

- We put the brightest geraniums we can find in pots and move them around as other plants come and go, so that there is always colour in all parts of the garden.
- Tall perennial grasses are inexpensive, fill in spaces with colour and texture, and provide year-round interest.
- When we get something new (particularly a gift or an impulse buy of a plant that is on sale and looks promising), we put it in the ground wherever there is a space, see what happens, and if it looks peaky, we move it.
- Our biggest success to date: A miniature rose that was a gift from someone and languished in the front garden until we found it a new home in a sunny space by the back wall and it grew like a triffid.
- It's thrifty gardening when you ask for plants as birthday presents and other gifts!

- **Dichondra** (*Dichondra argentea* 'Silver Falls') is a gorgeous, silvery, dripping-over-the-edge plant. It crawls all over a container, in sun or shade. This is another on my perfect plant list.
- **Sweet potato vine** (*Ipomoea batatas* 'Midnight Lace', or *I. b.* 'Sweet Caroline Bewitched Purple') is another magnificent dripper. Take cuttings for next year. Sun or part shade.
- **Anise sage, salvia** (*Salvia guaranitica* 'Black and Blue'). All salvias are lovely, but this one is a particularly intense blue and will get to a fair size by the end of summer (30 inches/75 cm). Needs sun.
- **Euphorbia** (*Euphorbia* 'Diamond Frost') is a froth of white in a little bit of shade, but will get very big and mounded with more sun.

Don't overwater annuals. It's the mistake many people make and they end up with a soggy, fungus-ridden mass. Or the plants get way too blowsy and fall over. Use the finger test to see if they really need watering. Or give them emergency watering the minute they start to droop.

Self-Seeding Annuals

Be careful of the following annuals. They *are* annuals, but they also may love your garden and seed themselves wherever the seed falls. If you have a small garden, they may spread far more widely than you actually have room for so, at the end of their blooming period, chop off their heads. If you like them, sprinkle the seed where you want to see them come back — but they'll do it on their own anyway.

- **Snow on the mountain** (*Euphorbia marginata*) has pretty grey and white blooms, but it will self-seed. You may want this but it can get into everything.
- **Tall verbena** (*Verbena bonariensis*) is a glorious see-through plant that will romp all over the place if the situation is right.
- **Cosmos** (*Cosmos* spp.) are sprightly creatures and you can let the ones you like best go to seed and pull out all the rest.
- **Candytuft** (*Iberis amara*) comes in so many colours, and as the year wears on, they all end up being a rather boring lavender. I love the white ones best, and for years I kept only those.
- **Forget-me-not** (*Myosotis alpestris*) is actually a biennial, which means it blooms every second year. But you can throw seeds around one year, do the same the next, and have them for a lifetime of pleasure.

VEGETABLES

Here are some delectable (and ornamental) vegetables and herbs that will work in a sunny garden or on a bright balcony.

- **Carrots:** They may take up a lot of room and be fussy to prick

out, but the taste of a homegrown carrot cannot be beat.
There are many heritage types available and the ferny tops
are amazingly decorative.

- **Greens:** From mesclun mixes to Asian greens, they offer a
startling range of colours and textures, given rich, moist soil.
- **Runner beans:** Grown up a teepee or obelisk, they are real
space-savers, and the flowers are magnets for bees and
hummingbirds.
- **Swiss chard:** Flavourful varieties with brilliantly coloured
stems will enhance any planting.
- **Basil:** A must-have herb, it has many new forms these days,
some purple, some with fabulous textured leaves. Taste it
before you buy it to make sure it's a plant you'd actually use.
- **Fennel:** This wonderful feathery herb will, if allowed, seed all
over the place, so be careful where you position it.
- **Curly parsley:** Easy to grow, it makes a terrific edging plant.
- **Rosemary:** Grow this shrubby herb in a terracotta pot for a
taste of Provence, or tuck it into any sunny border.

With the perennials Harvey Wrightman has suggested in his ten best
for sun and shade, you have a list of plants which will thrive in containers or very well-drained beds. Choose a few from there, a few from my
own list, add a couple of annuals and then a few seeds that will renew

themselves each year. You could make a fine garden of such a simple and straightforward plant list, but as you gain experience, you'll want to be more adventurous.

CHAPTER 5

THE PLANTING

O ver the decades my mantra has become: Tend to the soil first, then the garden will look after itself. Not quite, but close. One of the most expensive investments you *should* be making in the garden is preparing the soil properly. If you ignore this, it will be a largely wasted effort (and a waste of money) putting in a garden.

This first tenet of all thrifty gardening must be done with enthusiasm — not just sprinkling around a few bags of triple mix or compost. You must know your soil (what it's like right down to the texture) and how it drains. Ideal soil isn't too sandy or filled with too much clay — that nice friable middle ground called loam is what most plants enjoy. And make sure your good soil is at least 10 inches (25 cm) deep; 18 inches (45 cm) is better. Paying attention to this will pay off down the road.

SOIL

Soil is not only the essence of a good garden; it is the essence of life itself. We should have profound respect for this extremely complicated substance. It is comprised of billions of little creatures all at work, making it, not surprisingly, the most important material on earth. It takes 10,000 years to create an inch (2.5 cm) of soil, so think about that the next time you call it "dirt." The more you mess around with it, the more you disturb the profile it takes years to build. I'm a big believer in adding organic matter only to the soil surface and letting the worms and the natural microbial processes do the rest of the work. This saves an incredible amount of time and energy.

If you are nervous about the type of soil you have or unsure of what may have been dumped on it previously, get it tested. It's a complicated and expensive process, but there are effective home-testing kits, which are cheaper and can give you basic information about your soil. For a professional analysis, contact a local agricultural college, university, or garden school and ask where to send your soil samples. In the meantime, you can try the following on your own to determine one important aspect of your soil, the degree of acidity/alkalinity (called the pH):

- Dig up a bit of soil every 100 square feet (9.3 square metres) and mix it up in a bucket.
- Pour some vinegar on the soil sample. If nothing happens, the soil is probably acidic. But if it fizzles, it means there's a chemical reaction and you've got alkaline soil.

On the pH scale of 1 to 14, acidic soil is below 7, neutral soil is 7, and alkaline soil is above 7. Most plants — and soil organisms — thrive in a pH between 6.5 and 7, a neutral soil. But some species of plants prefer soils outside that range. For instance, rhododendrons and azaleas need acidic soil, which is created by the breakdown of needles and leaves from trees such as pines and oaks. It takes years for the soil to become more acidic. Alkaline soil is attractive to plants such as lilacs, clematis, and thyme. (Check out my book, *Ecological Gardening*, for more information about soil and its health). Check plant tags; they will tell you if you *must* have an acidic soil to grow. It's sensible to pay attention to this.

My sense of garden health is an over-all one: If it's looking good, it's probably in good shape. But if leaves droop, look too lacy, yellowed, or spotty, I'll swing into action. So a modicum of vigilance is always good; festering with worry never is.

HIGH-RISE SOIL PREP

Soil matters on the balcony garden just as it does on the ground. But the emphasis is different. It's about weight. How much weight is allowed on the balcony? Just how much can you haul up to your balcony alone? How much help will be needed? Think of all the stuff you'll need to get to the site: soil, compost, mulch, plants. What do you do with the empty containers afterward? Make sure there's a dolly available and, if you need it, book time on the service elevator. And, if you are in a new condo, make sure there *is* a service elevator (sounds hard to believe but too many designers have reported the lack of same).

The best soil I've used in balconies — because it holds plants in place, makes for good drainage, and needs topping up only once a year — is comprised of one-half reliable potting soil with one-half a combination of compost and well-composted bark. Mulch with the latter and most of the plants will thrive (the ones that fail have likely succumbed to the wind). You may have to experiment to get the soil composition exactly right. But here's one method:

1. Containers specially made for shrubs and perennials have to be at least 24 inches (60 cm) in diameter. Measure the size of the container to see how deep you want the soil to go.
2. Always leave an inch (2.5 cm) or so at the top.
3. Lay down a layer of potting soil 2 to 3 inches (5 to 8 cm) deep in the bottom.
4. Add a handful of a coir product (coir is one of the many coconut fibre-based products now on the market, and you may want to experiment with a couple to find the right one), which will help retain moisture.

5. Then add a layer of the compost-composted bark mix until you fill the container.
6. Add a final layer of mulch.

Top up your containers and raised beds with compost every spring, either by making your own or finding a really good one at a nursery. If you live in an enlightened city that has a composting program, fill a couple of heavy plastic bags for free at a local park on pick-up days. Store what you don't use immediately.

At the end of the season, any containers that don't have perennials in them should have all the soil dumped into one bag. Mix up the soil with fresh compost. You can even add your own vegetable parings and do some composting for the following spring — but only if you've got a place outside where you can leave the bag for the winter and it won't be unsightly. Poke some air holes in the side, and by spring everything will be composted down and ready to refill pots.

ALL YOU NEED TO KNOW ABOUT PLANTING

Planting should be fun. It's something you can do alone, with friends, with children, with someone who doesn't speak your language. It can be the calming Zen moment in a bad week. When you plant, you really can't be doing anything else, such as texting or talking on a cell phone. Personally, I can stand and watch a good planter go at it all day long and be giddy with the pleasure of watching a splendid performance.

Preparing to Plant

Sometimes in remaking a garden, it is wise to excavate a border completely. If the soil is practically solid clay, or riddled with concrete-like interlocking roots just below the surface, or has been fiendishly compacted by heavy machinery, you will have to put some serious muscle into getting it into friable (easily worked) shape.

Here are some useful tips:

- You'll need to dig down no less than 14 to 18 inches (35 cm to 45 cm) below grade. This will probably require manual help or someone with a backhoe, which can be expensive. But think long-range and realize that amortizing this work over several years will prove to be a good investment.

- Be sure you know where the excess soil is going to go. Must it be taken off site or can you salvage it? If you save it, be sure to mix it with a load of organic material and let it sit a while before using it again.

- Measure the area for soil replacement. Multiply length by width by depth to get cubic footage and then divide by 27 to get the number of cubic yards. (This formula works for containers as well.)

- Make certain that any new soil is good quality (not stuff that has been hauled out of a farmer's field — such soil could be full of ground-up corn and weeds or doused with chemicals). Also, any manure you bring in should be well composted, i.e., looks and feels like lovely soil, and doesn't smell. Fresh manure is too hot and will damage plants.

Whether you are planting a new garden from scratch, renovating an existing one, or simply doing some fine-tuning, it helps to divide the garden into sections — even if this is just a mental exercise — and tackle each area separately with the long-range idea of knitting them together into one glorious sweep.

Here is a necessary step-by-step process for preparing your garden for planting:

1. Familiarize yourself with what you have, and clean out weeds, dead or dying plants, and stuff you know you don't want.

2. Get a good arborist to limb up trees and get helpers to cut down unwanted trees or weed trees. Cut back shrubs for better shape. The idea is to get more light into any space that's overgrown. Untrammelled growth is often just plain ugly.

3. If you are revamping an entire area, dig up plants to be saved (except large trees and shrubs), repot and water them, and set them to one side. Once again, don't be sentimental about plants. They will compost down and evolve to live another day, another way.

4. Dig over the area to get rid of roots, stones and any junk (astonishing what people bury in their backyards apart from dogs, cats, and gerbils). Dig down to a minimum of 8 inches

(20 cm) and as deep as 18 inches (45 cm). You'll need this much depth for the root run of most plants. (Big trees may need deeper holes, depending on the size of their rootballs.) If necessary, replace horrible soil with new good-quality soil.

5. Amend the soil with organic matter such as leaf mould, well-rotted manure, or compost (I use duck compost). Do this with any planting area, large or small.

6. Put the potted plants in the planting space or spaces, and arrange them in different combinations until you have a satisfying design. Take time doing this; even a few inches one way or another can make a huge difference in the aesthetic response. Once they're set, rotate each one to find its best "face" (a side that looks better than all the others; every plant has one, very much like people). I usually check this by sitting in what I imagine is the client's favourite spot and where the plant will be seen most of the time.

7. Put any useless plants on the compost heap or, failing that, on the curb for someone else to enjoy.

When I'm asked to come to a garden consultation, often these basic steps are all that's required. A new set of eyes will see the value of what already exists and will also see almost immediately how to repurpose or reposition plants to give even the simplest garden a whole new look. You will be astonished at how a garden can be completely made over using this technique.

If you have doubts about your ability to place plants properly, hire a professional. In the long run, a good one will save you money and you'll get much more long-term satisfaction with the results.

Planting Techniques

I'd like to say that I always know where I'm going to place a plant and have a perfect hole ready and waiting, but it's seldom that simple. What usually happens is that I wander around with each new plant, trying it here and trying it there to see where it fits in. Some plants are so ideal for a specific spot that others will be moved around to make room for it. The excellence of your choices in tools really pays off here. Use a shovel for a big hole, a trowel for small perennials, annuals, and bulbs.

Here are some guidelines to follow when you're ready to plant:

- Plant early in the morning or wait until the evening when the temperature has cooled off.
- Always dig a hole that's as deep as the root system of the plant and slightly wider.
- Water the hole. Make sure that the water is absorbed by the soil.
- Bang the plant out of the container (this won't hurt the plant).
- Fluff up the roots with your hands. By "fluffing up the roots" I mean pull them firmly but gently apart until they fan out nicely into the bottom of the hole. This technique will allow

PLANTING TIPS

Careful prep can make a very nice garden into something brilliant. Seeing well-grown plants is profound. It hits you right in the solar plexis. Here's how to get that feeling.

- When you order new soil, look for a mix of loam, a bit of sand, plus organic matter such as compost and manure.
- Let new or freshly dug soil settle before you start planting. It will sink a bit so take that into consideration.
- Here's a tip from organic gardener Lorraine Robertson: When you plant, add mycorrhizal fungi to the planting hole; they will help the plant to take water and nutrients from the soil. That is what happens in nature.
- Give your plants a good start with lots of water until they are established and then they should take care of themselves. Don't spoil them.

the roots to spread out properly in the soil. And if you feel you are stuffing the plant into the hole, make it wider still but, again, not much deeper than the root system.

- Carefully place the plant into the hole.
- Fill the hole with soil.
- Press the soil down gently around the plant so there are no air pockets.
- Add compost around the plant and water everything slowly and deeply. Do it by hand or move a hose that's on a low drib-

ble around the base of the plants. It's this attention to detail that will help maintain your plants' health.

Sandra Pella, head gardener at Toronto Botanical Garden, spent time training at Great Dixter, Christopher Lloyd's magnificent garden in England. Here's what she recommends:

- When planting a bed, always plant from the outside in. First, spread the plants around in your design. Then begin planting from the front of the border and work your way in — not the other way around. We always did this when I worked with the City, and it was confirmed for me at Great Dixter. This technique helps prevent the soil from compacting before you plant — as you move from front to the back, you won't disturb anything behind you because it's already been planted and helps to avoid excess compaction by walking all over the soil.
- When planting with a trowel, begin by digging the hole with the trowel in your right hand (or left hand if you're left-handed), and with your left insert the plant in the hole. Then use both hands to move the soil into the planting hole and press down.
- Work one section at a time. Complete all tasks — cutting back; lifting and dividing; adding soil and compost; replanting; adding a fresh layer of mushroom or regular compost — before moving on to the next bed.

- Always work on boards, especially if the soil has been over-worked and compacted. Kneeling on boards distributes your weight evenly over a greater surface area.
- "Tickle" the soil. Whenever leaving a bed, the last task is always to go over the soil lightly with a long-handled, three-pronged tool, and fluff up the top inch or so of soil to avoid compaction.

I love planting because it makes me feel like I'm participating in the natural evolution of the garden. Even if you hire someone else to do it because you can't yourself, watch what's being done, enjoy this part of the process. And never fear if you change your mind later on. Most plants are pretty tough and don't mind moving.

Also, don't worry if your newly planted border looks a bit raw at first. If you've grouped your plants by colour or texture, you can see almost immediately what else should be added. But don't rush into finishing a job that generally takes a long time to mature. Gaps can be temporarily filled with annuals that complement the perennials (pick up a colour from bloom or leaf).

Remember that thrifty gardening is ultimately slow gardening. It might take a few years for the thrifty garden to reveal its true beauty.

GROWING VEGETABLES

Much has been made of vegetable gardening in recent years and the blither is deafening. What you should be looking for is some fun and a little bit of food. Sometime trends like this make gardeners competitive, but it might also fulfill the need to get closer to how our food is grown. It's the perfect way to get children interested in food production and gardening.

Here's what you need:

♦ **Boards** to kneel/stand on (see what Sandra Pella says about planting and boards page 122). This is doubly true when planting seeds.
♦ **Well-prepared soil.**
♦ **Stakes and string** so that you can plant seeds in a nice straight line and organize a method of regular watering. And read what the seed package says about how deeply you plant the seed.

Or you can start seeds separately with:

♦ **A container (soup can, wooden box)**; make sure it has drainage holes in the bottom.
♦ Clunk in some compost or rich soil and add the seeds.
♦ Water the seeds but don't overwater. A mister always works well.

♦ Once the plants start sprouting, you will see how many need to be thinned out.

That's it. Keep on watering (use the finger test: stick your finger into the soil up to the second knuckle; if it comes out dry, water). BUT (and once again here's that caveat) vegetables need six to eight hours of sunlight a day. If your garden or balcony doesn't have access to that much sunlight, move on to growing other kinds of plants.

If you intend to have a vegetable garden, prepping the soil is an absolute must, as is good drainage. So be prepared to do lots of prep, as well as watering. You cannot have a vegetable garden without watering it regularly by hand.

There is one great trend I love today and that's mixing vegetables into perennial borders. There are so many sensual, glamorous vegetables — kale and Swiss chard are just two examples — that it makes me long to have more sun in my garden. Purple basil, fennel, and rosemary would be there for sure. There are some glorious examples of these combinations in containers, in front gardens, and in traditional borders. This is actually a revival of the very old cottage garden so admired by Gertrude Jekyll, the doyenne of English garden designers and writers. She saw the beauty in humble workers' gardens and enhanced their ideas to bring about a revolution in garden design.

Growing Vegetables in Balcony Containers

Lara Lucretia Mrosovsky, along with the Hincks-Dellcrest Centre and

Green Thumbs Growing Kids, has set up a wonderful gardening program in the high rises of downtown Toronto. Lara and her co-workers have helped hundreds of families get started with balcony gardening in St. James Town. Here are a few suggestions from Lara's charming booklet called *An Illustrated Guide to Growing Food on Your Balcony*. She encourages gardeners looking for containers to scrounge the neighbourhood, from winemaking outlets and corner stores to the recycling bins at nurseries.

She says, "Large plants that need large pots are cucumbers, eggplants, ground cherries, potatoes, tomatillos, and tomatoes. Big containers are for a single large fruiting plant or for multiple small plants." Here are some vegetable containers that she recommends:

- **A half barrel** is the minimum size for raspberries or currants. Try asking wine-making supply stores, vineyards, or nurseries.
- **A bushel basket** can be lined with a plastic bag (drill holes in the bottom).
- **A recycling bin or plastic tub** is excellent for one or two large plants.
- **A five-gallon bucket** usually accommodates just one large plant (drill holes in the bottom).
- **A soap bucket** is great for one large plant (drill holes in the bottom).
- **Buckets used for kitty litter.**

- ◆ **Milk crates or shopping baskets** have lots of holes in them. Line with burlap or landscaping cloth. A milk crate fits one large plant or several small ones. Handles make it easy to move.

Lara recommends growing chili peppers on balconies because they thrive in smaller pots (with rich soil) and produce well all season long without full sun. You can even move your chili pepper inside for the winter and then start next spring with a fully grown plant.

Lara's Top 5 Thrifty Tips for Balcony Vegetable Gardening:

1. **Use recycled containers.** There's no need to purchase expensive new ones, when large containers can be found in the recycling every day! Even the recycling bins themselves can be useful for growing.

2. **Save your own seed.** In addition to saving seed from your balcony favourites each year, check out the kitchen — from sweet peppers to mung beans (for sprouts), to fruits like pears, avocado, or citrus, and roots like potatoes or sweet potatoes. You can even regrow the bottom of leeks or a cabbage stem, and get new tasty leaves.

3. **Make your own compost.** Construct a simple composter or use a worm bin (it fits into a small space and doesn't smell). Compost is rich, organic plant food, and if you make it yourself out of discarded veggie and fruit scraps, it's practically free.

4. **Grow foods that are expensive to buy.** For instance, herbs like rosemary, cilantro, or basil cost about $3 per bunch (more for organic), and often the bunches are too big to use all at once. Why not spend your $3 on a package of seeds — you'll have fresh herbs all season long and you can pick just the right amount for a meal.

5. **Make cuttings and share them among friends.** This money-saving tactic works beautifully for mint, oregano, thyme, and basil, to name a few.

Containers and sun are a great combination for a lovely little garden. If you've ever watched the enchanting TV chef Jamie Oliver, you'll see him putting seeds in just about anything, from a tin can to an old rubber boot. But be sure you want to spend the time with the plants. They will need water every day (sometimes twice a day depending on your sun exposure); they will need a little bit of thinning out (you can always nibble what you prick out); and of course you must be prepared to eat the harvest.

Most herbs are going to find balcony containers a good place to grow. They like sun and are drought tolerant: basil, oregano, summer savory, marjoram, thyme (there are lots of different kinds, including lemon, orange, and caraway). But remember, keep containers planted with vegetables out of the wind. Buy smaller varieties of tomatoes and look for dwarf cultivars of carrots, eggplant, lettuces, and greens. Try out the different kinds of Swiss chard — all are gorgeous as well as delicious.

THRIFTY TREE TIP

Gardener Blaine Marchand who gardens in the country has this thrifty tree tip:

Being in the country, one can choose truly large specimens not even comprehensible in the city. It is best to purchase quality trees from a nursery rather than dig them out of nearby woods where, protected by other trees, the bark is sheltered from strong winds and late winter strong sun. Placed suddenly in solitary confinement, the epidermis alternatively thaws during the day and freezes through the night, resulting in severe winter cracking. Nursery sales throughout the summer offer great savings for larger trees.

PLANTING TREES

No garden can survive without trees. We need them to clean the air, support wildlife, and give vertical interest to a design. And they are the best and most efficient of air conditioners anywhere. The air around a big tree will be 10°C cooler than out in the blazing sun.

But be cautious in choosing trees, and be very particular. Well planted, a tree will last long after you do; badly planted, it's an expensive item to rescue or get rid of.

The best advice I've ever been given was to always *plant proud*. It means having the base of the trunk (where it will ultimately flare out with age), slightly above the surface of the soil. If you sink the base into a hole, the water drains into the depression and the chance of rot setting in is likely.

Here is a step-by-step plan on *planting proud* trees and shrubs:

The Hole

Digging a proper hole requires a deeply dished shovel with a long handle to do the job efficiently. A hole has to be custom dug; every tree will be different in its requirements.

- Dig a hole the same depth as and about twice as wide as the rootball (use a shovel as your measuring stick).
- Use only the soil that comes from the hole itself if it's in good condition, then add some top dressing (organic material) later. Recently, I've been throwing in a handful of a product containing mycorrhizae, beneficial fungi that help plants take up nutrients. It also seems to boost the plant's ability to withstand uncertain winter weather, which seems the norm these days. The product resembles dried-up kitty litter, so it's easy to use.
- Set the rootball in the hole ensuring it's not sitting too low, and fill the hole halfway with soil, pressing it firmly around the rootball. Water it if there are a lot of spaces in the roots (you want to eliminate any air pockets).
- Fill the rest of the hole, and top dress around the tree with manure, compost, or a mix of the two, keeping it well away from the bark.
- Water slowly and thoroughly (see below).

The Water

Water, water everywhere and not a drop going to the root system of plants. That's how most people water when they fling it about with the hose or leave the sprinkler or watering system on for a few minutes every day. Pointless waste of a precious resource. Do it properly or hire someone who can.

- Set the hose at a dribble and put the mouth at the drip line of the tree or shrub. Move it around so that each part of the root zone gets watered very deeply and very slowly, and the soil below the root system can absorb the water.

- Do the dribbling twice a week for three months and usually the tree will look after itself after that. But keep a keen eye on the tree and stick your finger in the ground for the knuckle test (dry to the second knuckle), or get a water meter.

- Sprinklers are not efficient at getting water below the roots because some of the water is lost to evaporation and more is deflected by the leaves. You must get below the canopy of even the smallest plants.

- Watering should be done on a regular basis when it doesn't rain. An established tree will be able to get along with what nature provides (unless there's a heat wave); then it needs a regular three-bucket dump at least twice a week. See Chapter 7 for everything you need to know about watering.

The Mulch

Mulch is necessary for all North American gardens. It is the blanket of life in these days of uncertain weather or wild shifts in temperature. It will ensure the root systems of plants aren't subjected to freeze-thaw cycles and will keep the temperature underground even. It holds in moisture, breaks down slowly, and feeds the plants at the same time.

- Apply mulch at least once a year, preferably twice (early spring and late autumn).
- Mulch eventually breaks down, feeding the soil. You can go to the expense of buying fertilizer spikes, but save the money. Good mulch, along with compost tea, manure tea, and a plain feed of compost do a terrific job.
- Don't pile up mulch against the trunk of the tree; otherwise it will encourage rot or attract animals. See Chapter 7 for more on mulch.

The Surround

What you put around trees can be almost as important as how you plant them, not just for its look in a design but especially for plant health. You don't want to interfere with the flare, which is critical to a tree's health.

- Always choose shallow-rooted ground covers to plant near a tree or shrub.

TIPS FOR TREES AND SHRUBS

Nick Palumbo is a professional gardener who would never consider removing a shrub if there was any possibility of transforming it. Why buy new when you can fix old? Here are some of his thrifty tips:

- Instead of cutting down a tree casting way too much shade into or threatening a small garden, trim it back to a height of between 15 and 20 feet (4.5 and 6 m). It will grow out, but at this height it's easy to control.

- Use smaller trees. You can still blot out your neighbours, but you won't be cutting out your own light. A tree should draw your eyes up. Look up the trunk and if it's pleasing to your eye, keep it. It's how you create antiquity in your garden.

- If you have a shrub or even an unruly vine, espalier it along the fence. Do this with even the most boring of forsythias: Cut out all but a few long stalks, pin them along the fence, and watch them bloom outrageously. Since they bloom on new wood (the stuff that grows this year), cut them back for the following year.

- If you want a tree-cum-hedge effect for privacy, plant inexpensive cedars close together and then clip the branches off the trunks from the ground upward to 4 or 5 feet (1.2 to 1.5 m), creating a "hedge on stilts." You can also do this with Bradford pear (*Pyrus calleryana* 'Bradford'), which is cheap, columnar, has flowers in spring, fruit for birds, and leaves that are the last to fall in autumn.

- Dwarf crab apple trees are often scorned because they sucker. But if you bury the graft, it won't sucker. They make good espaliers and have many shades of bloom.

- Sycamore and linden trees also respond well to heavy pruning.

♦ If you make a cedar hedge and clip the lower 3 feet (1 m), it's possible to grow an understorey of bulbs and daylilies. Even roses will grow up cedars as long as the cedars are kept under control.

♦ Never let trees grow to be taller than your highest ladder; that way you can always get up on the ladder and trim the tree back to scale.

♦ Don't plant smack dab up against any tree. If you are dealing with ancient trees but want to add a bit of colour to the area safely, plant between the flare with shallow-rooted plants. Use native plants that have spent eons evolving this symbiosis.

♦ Don't plop trees and shrubs into the middle of a grass sward. It's like putting them in green cement, and they stand the chance of getting hit by a lawn mower or whipper-snipper. By the same token, it doesn't help either the ground cover or woody plants to have them too close together. Most trees and shrubs need a healthy space (a good 18 inches/45 cm), relatively free of ground cover, around the base. Some plants will snuggle up, but haul them out if they bother the tree.

♦ Don't let ivy and other vines nip up the bark of a tree. It can be starved of needed sunlight for photosynthesis, and even strangled. This, of course, is one of those controversial topics, so pick your side.

The Pruning

Pruning can be the frugal gardener's best tactic for saving money and making the garden look fantastic. It's worthwhile to take a pruning course, buy a well-illustrated book, or hire a pro to do it while you lurk nearby and watch. Always use recently sharpened, clean tools (wiped off with denatured alcohol). Here are a few useful tricks:

- Never make a cut flat against the bark of a woody plant. There should be enough of a slant to keep the cut slightly away from the trunk or branch but close enough so that a callus will develop around the wound and heal itself.
- Don't leave a stub sticking out. Diseases and insects can enter a stub easily and damage the plant. It's also a sure sign of sloppy technique.
- Never use plant paint to "dress the wound." It's not only pointless, but will also inhibit the plant's ability to heal itself.
- Coppicing: Many shrubs can be coppiced, i.e., cut to about 3 inches (8 cm) from the ground. Toss out the dead stuff but keep the good-looking stems. This is a dandy way to acquire free twigs for your urns, as well as making attractive plant props. Store them in a decent container and this in itself is decorative. They can be used for years and save you from buying stakes.
- Pleaching: This pruning tactic produces a hedge on lollipop sticks: Bare legs with growth at the top. It's a fantastic way

to make a screen within the garden or at the edges. Trees are planted relatively close together and then the branches are trained to grow into each other's arms. The lower part of the tree trunks are kept clear of branches. The English use horizontal metal forms to do the training. However, you can select trees with a natural penchant for sideways growth and trim them every year to get a similar effect, with a good deal less mucking about. In spring, cut back anything that isn't on a horizontal line and trim the horizontal stems, so you have the permanent structure. Do this front and back to create a narrow profile. (It looks and acts a lot like espalier, which involves training a tree or shrub flat against a wall or lattice.) Both an espalier and a pleached hedge can make a wonderful green screen. Trees for pleaching: Hornbeam (*Carpinus* spp.), crab apple (*Malus* spp.), and beech (*Fagus sylvestris*).

- Pollarding: This is a brutal form of pruning. You see it in Europe all the time: The tree branches are pruned annually right back to "bare knuckles" — where branches sprout from the top of the trunk. Then each spring, they resprout from these cuts. It prevents the trees from getting too big and keeps them the shape you want. But it must be done every year, and you should really decide to do it from the time the tree is planted.

- Prune deciduous trees during the winter or while still dormant and before buds begin to swell up.

10 DUMB THINGS PEOPLE DO WITH TREES

One person who feels the same way I do about the sanctity of trees is arborist Derek Welsh, whom I admire intensely and who has strong, sometimes controversial opinions. So what does he think about how we treat trees? Here, in no particular order, are the top 10 arboreal crimes he sees people commit.

1. Put holiday lights in trees.
2. Empty pool water under trees.
3. Plant trees too deeply.
4. Plant trees under any kind of wires.
5. Make improper cuts, mainly too close to the cambium.
6. Build fences and decks to trees.
7. Plant trees too close to buildings.
8. Wrap wire or ropes around trees for any reason.
9. Plant the wrong tree in the wrong location.
10. Till at the base of the tree.

♦   Prune most evergreens in late winter or early spring when you can see the damage the snow and frost has done. If there are lots of brown needles, brush them off wearing a pair of leather gloves. You never know — they might grow back nicely. Wait to prune fir, spruce, and pine, which should be pruned after new growth has begun.

- ◆ Don't prune when there's a drought or when too many needles or leaves have been lost to disease or infestations.
- ◆ Always prune for shape and take out any dead or crossing branches.

I love trees and it's painful to see people not caring for them as the magnificent creatures they are. They will reward you for generations, keep you cool and safe, and surround you in beauty. How could we not look after them carefully?

RAISED BEDS FOR A THRIFTIER GARDEN

In countries like Japan, where space is at a premium, almost all the gardens are comprised of raised beds — beds or borders raised above the ground to a height of 6 inches (15 cm) or more. They are amazingly flexible because they save a huge amount of effort in performing garden chores. They warm up earlier in spring; you control the drainage, which can make or break plant health, and vastly expands the number of plants available to use; they are easier to access and save a lot of bending over; and just about all plants love them.

For instance, raised beds are ideal for alpines, which originate high up in mountainous regions. Adapting to such difficult climates has made them incredibly tough and absolutely gorgeous. They require a minimum of care and usually bloom when nothing else is around, which is a boon to gardeners in the far north.

Nurseryman Harvey Wrightman learned not only to love raised-bed gardening while working with alpine plants, but also to make troughs or raised beds with a material called tufa, a soft porous rock full of minerals. These tufa troughs can be turned into miniature gardens (ideal for balconies). Trough plants are eye-openers: Splashy, marvellous colour, exquisite little bits of delicious sights.

Here, Harvey explains what you need to make a crevice garden in a trough or raised bed:

Soil: The best soils are *garden soil*–based — basically, mineral with a little organic matter added. The organic matter breaks down after two years and strange things happen chemically/biologically. Green roof people have discovered this, too. Their mixes are based on "expanded shales," a non-toxic, porous material manufactured by Norlite. This product was originally made for use in lightweight concrete, but has horticultural uses as well. A typical "green roof" mix will contain mostly expanded shale and 6 percent organic matter, which might be coir or compost. Nutrition is provided by a slow-release fertilizer: I add 25 percent Spanish River Carbonatite (SRC), which is both soil and slow-release fertilizer. It is a stable, long-lasting source of nutrition, which eliminates the use of artificial fertilizer.

Construction: The great Czech plantsman, Josef Halda, showed me how to make a raised bed from a clay-crevice construction. First, he selects tufa chunks that can be split into two or three pieces. These will form the basic crevices. The breaks are clean and angular, making it easy to bring pieces closely together. For a trough, one piece can be split into two or three pieces. These pieces are book-matched and will form the basic crevice in between two pieces of the material.

The Basics: The narrow quarter-to-half-inch (6 to 12 mm) crevice is filled with a very sticky clay mix. The slabs are glued together with a paste made of clay and sand. I use bagged masons or refractory clay from a hobby store. Three parts of clay to one part sand, mixed until it forms a sticky paste.

- Using a flat spatula, apply the paste to one side of the crevice to just under half an inch (10 mm) thickness.
- The roots of the transplant are then splayed on the surface and the two pieces of the tufa, which form the crevice, are then brought together. In this way, you are providing a large surface area for the roots, and the clay line retains a more constant moisture level. Although watering is required, the plant itself never gets soggy because it is elevated.
- The plants can be placed in vertical constructions with the slices of tufa forming what look like "cliffs" — to give more visual drama. By using more mat-forming plants to stabilize the soil lines from eroding away, you can then interplant with several different kinds of plants and their root systems won't interfere with each other.

To give yourself some training on this method of planting, have a look at the wonderful video on Harvey's website, www.wrightman alpines.com. It shows Josef Halda fashioning a crevice garden on a grand scale. But it can be interpreted for any size of trough or raised bed or even on a micro scale for a balcony.

PLANTING OFF THE GROUND

Planting on a balcony or terrace means container gardening, which is another form of making a garden in raised beds. You are planting off the ground and the same good things can happen — the best of which is having the soil warm up earlier in spring.

The Containers

- The first rule of all container planting is that the container must have a hole in the bottom. If the water can't drain out, you'll have a swamp and dying plants.
- The second rule is to match the container with the plant's root size: Big plants need big containers; shallow containers will hold only shallow-rooted plants properly. Most of the plants you'll be dealing with will be annuals, which usually have fairly shallow root systems, especially most of the vegetables. This means you don't need giant containers to hold them. And, of course, the bigger the container the more expensive it will be.

The Planting

- Use a potting soil, plus amendments such as manure or compost when you plant in a container. Soak the potting mix so that it has absorbed enough water before you put it into the containers. Add a slow-release fertilizer if you need to, but follow the instructions. More is NOT better.
- Plant late in the day when the sun is off your space.
- Soak plants in a bucket or the bathtub before popping them into place (get a filter to keep the soil out of the drain).
- Toss a handful of coir product on the bottom, followed by a handful of a product that contains mycorrhizal fungi. Mycorrhizae will help bind with the roots and produce healthy plants, and will add lots of life to your soil. This is especially important with perennials such as shrubs and trees.
- Fill about two-thirds of the container with soil.
- Place your preferred plant combination on top of the soil, and move them around until you've got the right plant in the right place.
- Adjust the height as needed so that the loosened rootballs are covered with soil, and the tops are the same level as your final level of soil, which should be at least an inch (2.5 cm) below the lip of the container.

HIGH-RISE GARDEN PROBLEMS

Pauline and Ian lived in their dream home — a midtown Victorian house with huge granite stone steps leading down to a terraced garden with a wisteria-covered pergola, a parking pad, and many different nooks to wander into.

Pauline, however, had a terrible accident and was left confined to crutches and often to a wheelchair. Drastic circumstances, of course, call for drastic action. When Ian returned home after an overnight trip during which she felt trapped in her office by a fear of the stairs, she said it took him less than twenty-four hours to say, "Okay, we'll find a condo." And what they found was exactly the opposite of what they had before. "But we are gifted for happiness," Pauline explains. "People who cling desperately to the past cannot be happy."

They found a sunlit condo right in the middle of downtown Toronto with generous balconies and a comfortable living space. They wanted a garden outside to enhance an office, huge dining/living room, and the guest bedroom so each part of the 600-square-foot (56-square-metre) balcony had to have some special purpose.

To get a magnificent garden was a complicated affair. The higher the balcony, of course, the more garden problems will surface, and they were on the fortieth floor with a space swept by relentless winds roughly three hundred days a year. Not to mention the blazing sunshine.

We hired Box Design to create special containers that worked with the scale of the balcony, and flooring to give it slightly different levels, plus a watering system. Various areas of the balcony were covered with cedar decking to give a humane contrast to the concrete. And lighting artist Pam Bingham gave the balcony her own touch of magic.

We tried radical things to get plants to grow in these extreme conditions. We filled the lightweight containers as quickly as we could so the soil wouldn't blow away, and then hoped for the best with an experimental watering system and patient owners. The growing medium we used was a combination of good soil mixed with some coir, compost, and well-composted pine bark. (We found this worked fine for two years but it needed annual topping up to keep the soil lively.)

The plants had to be tough and compact to stand up to the conditions, and to avoid obstructing those astounding views. So we used plants rated for Zones 2 or 3, such as alpine plants and low shrubs of known hardiness, and experimented with rugged, rock-garden-type plants, mountain plants, plants born to be assaulted by the elements.

The great triumphs were the tough-as-nails but delicate-looking buckthorn, *Rhamnus frangula* 'Fine Line' (a plant no longer commercially available). Hellebores did astoundingly well. We even had an area dubbed "The Farm," where Pauline could grow her herbs — lavenders for scent, and rosemary for cooking cherry tomatoes. Vines struggled because of the wind. *Clematis fargesioides*, a particularly rambunctious vine on the ground, popped up blooming its face off but grew to about one-third its normal size.

Boxwood was amazing and added what solid green we could get. The surprising thing was an ornamental weeping silver pear (*Pyrus salicifolia* 'Pendula'). This is one of my favourite trees and I thought it would have a tough time. It has survived, though it won't get huge (7 feet/2.1 m, about half its normal size). Its silvery foliage complements perfectly the sitting area outside Pauline's office.

One huge success was an annual Egyptian papyrus (*Cyperus papyrus*) called 'King Tut', which we'll use each year because it gets quite large. Grasses such as Japanese forest grass (*Hakonechloa macra* 'All Gold' and *H. m.* 'Aureola') also did exceptionally well.

All gardens are an experiment, but a balcony garden is more so simply because each element it must endure is so extreme. It's hard to retrain your gardener's eye to such a confined area but the balcony garden, suspended in space, has incredible thrills.

Balcony and terrace gardening come with their own problems as well as pleasures. But how much better is it to look out through some lovely plants either framing or blocking the view outside, rather than being surrounded by cement.

KEEPING TRACK OF PLANTS

Planting the right plant in the right place is one of the thriftiest ways of making a garden. It does mean you've got to do some research about the plants you would like to grow. The Internet has made this much easier for all of us, but be diligent and double-check anything you uncover. There's a lot of misinformation floating about and repeated. Even with good research, you still can't be absolutely sure how a plant will perform in your unique space. You must read tags before you put a plant into the soil and it's always a good idea to record what you've done. Here's a simple method of keeping track:

- Put all the tags into a bag with the year recorded on the outside.
- Record every plant purchased that year on a long-running computer list.
- Organize the list in alphabetical order by botanical name, followed by the common name; that way a search can be done either way.
- Keep a record of what the plants cost, how well each plant does, if and when it dies, and when it had to be replaced. This will help organize your plant budget from year to year.

This is one thrifty habit to develop. I tend to record all my perennials, certainly the trees and shrubs, in a computer file that's now running more than thirty single-spaced pages. I don't remove plants from the list when they die because it's interesting to know what didn't work over the years.

This kind of list is way better than having a plant map of your garden, because you'll likely move stuff around and forget to record what and where on the map. You will astound yourself by the number of plants you buy, and checking to see how much you paid for them over the years is fascinating. You can follow how you evolve as a gardener as well. It's like writing your very own gardening book. Eventually you'll end up with a record of how your taste has changed over the years, what you'd never allow into the garden ever again, and what you long for. We are quirky, we gardeners. So don't expect consistency.

Plants are the heart and soul of gardening. Treating them individually with the respect that all nature deserves will make you a much happier and contented person. Working with what nature gives us and helping to improve it with sensitivity and care will make wherever you garden a better place than how you found it. Stewardship is everyone's responsibility.

CHAPTER 6

THE THRIFTY
PROPAGATOR

I talk to many experienced gardeners in the course of a given year. When I ask, "What's your best thrifty garden tip?" they shout, "Learn how to propagate." When Tony Avent, who has one of the biggest mail order nurseries in the world, says it (after all, it's his business to sell plants), we must pay attention.

To propagate means you make new plants — by dividing plants; rooting stems; layering plants (weighing a nicked branch down on the ground and allowing it to grow new roots); sowing seeds either in pots or directly in the ground; and growing plants that will spew seeds all about to produce new plants on their own (self-seeding). You can make woody cuttings (taking a twig and putting it in sand to root) and even grow trees and shrubs from seed (a process not for the faint of heart because it can take years and years to do). There is no end to the variations on propagation but, like all aspects of gardening, it takes many hours of experimenting and patience to build up skills. And there's a mystique that keeps this chore from attracting the gardening novice: It sounds too difficult; it's just for the pros. As this chapter will tell you, this is definitely not true. Anyone can propagate and to do so will fill out borders very quickly at very low cost or for nothing. Now that's thrifty.

PROPAGATING FROM SEED

Growing or propagating from seed can be daunting but even if you don't become a devotee, give it a whirl at least once. There is something truly profound watching a large plant emerge from a tiny seed.

The other pleasure of seeds is the fact that there are dozens of astounding seed catalogues to tempt the most jaded of souls. Such catalogues and a seed list (more on that) can be among your thriftiest garden investments, not only through the seeds themselves but also for the valuable information they contain. You can get a solid horticultural education from seed catalogues, especially those from plant societies. They're an absolute gold mine, as are some of the society websites.

I belong to the Ontario Rock Garden and Hardy Plant Society, and when the Seedex (seed exchange) list comes in, it's straight to the bathtub for hours of fantasy reading. No pictures here, just list and lists of the wonderful seeds that members have gathered and are offering to other members. When I go through the lists of plants, I realize what I already have and, more important, how many plants I don't have and should look up.

It costs very little to join one of these garden communities (about the price of a good plant). They usually have regular meetings and, often, a journal. Terrific sources of local knowledge, these publications contain fantastic amounts of collected wisdom about much-loved plants by people who live in your area and who have first-hand experience growing the plants. All these gardeners fling themselves into these projects with mixed but never less than interesting results.

Years ago, I'd order lots of seeds but these days, unless I'm going to team up with someone else (who will grow the seeds with me so we really do end up with good plants), I try a few, very select ones. At this society it's possible for members to choose sixty packets of seeds for a mere $15 — a real bargain and a serious temptation to buy, buy, buy.

Every region in North America has a rock garden society, and there are societies for practically every plant as well as plant parts. I'm kidding about the latter but it's close. There is no weird aspect of gardening that doesn't have like-minded gardeners who have formed a group to exchange information and share their love of plants. Join up. It's a garden dollar well spent.

I have a tendency to get more catalogues than I could possibly ever need. But I know I'll find something I long for. In many, the photography is good enough to give a pretty good idea of what the plants will look like. As well you get detailed instructions on the plant's needs:

light, soil, and watering conditions. Already you are making inroads on decisions about how much you want to spend and where you'll put your garden dollar. And, you haven't invested a penny on gas.

What follows is a list a wonderful plants that are all easily grown from seed. Dugald Cameron (www.gardenimport.com) made this selection, and he adds his reasons for his choices:

- **Delphinium** (*Delphinium*): A snap to grow from seed. Don't thin out the weak seedlings if the seed is a mixture of colours. The weaker seedlings may provide the choicest colours.
- **Coneflower** (*Echinacea* spp.): Coneflowers are natives and attract bumblebees. Both the annual and perennial types are good from seed, though the very latest varieties are probably only available as plants.
- **Rose campion** (*Lychnis coronaria*): This has silky grey foliage and eyeball-searing magenta blooms.
- **Columbine** (*Aquilegia* spp.): This plant will hybridize itself as you attract more and more insects into the garden.
- **Foxglove** (*Digitalis purpurea*): An excellent cutting plant. The toxicity is highly exaggerated.
- **Forget-me-nots** (*Myosotis* spp.): You can't have a garden without them and, once you have seeded them, you have them for life. Just yank out the ones that you've placed in the wrong spot.
- **Candytuft** (*Iberis sempervirens*): This flower's blooms change from white to pink to lilac.

- **Perennial sweet pea** (*Lathyrus vernus*): Perennial sweet pea has a huge seed and is easy to handle. Best to soak the seed overnight before planting.
- **Pot marigold** (*Calendula*): A must-have annual because it's pretty, self-sows, and is easy to control.
- **Tall verbena** (*Verbena bonariensis*): A nice "see-through" annual that self-sows and is easy to control.

Growing plants from seed has pleasures all of its own. You can be proud of something you had a hand in right from its inception. The feeling of ownership is quite amazing, especially the first time you produce something downright glorious.

Sowing Perennial Seeds

Doug Green not only makes his living as a garden writer, but also sells plants. Here is his step-by-step guide for starting perennial seeds on the ground:

1. In autumn cut the bottom off a 6-inch pot (or even larger) — anything smaller tends to be more difficult to water.
2. Sink pots into the soil so that only the top inch (2.5 cm) of the rim is above ground.
3. Sterilize the soil inside the pot by slowly pouring boiling hot water over it. This will kill all seeds in the pot. The more hot water you use, the better.

4. Allow the soil to cool.

5. Sow the seeds and cover them with soil to protect them from mice/ants and from drying out. Do NOT cover them deeply, just enough so the seed disappears.

6. Walk away for the winter. Leave the seeds to Mother Nature.

7. In spring, transplant the germinated seeds.

Sowing Annual Seeds

You can use almost anything — egg cartons are good — to sow annual seeds in. Start them early in spring and make sure the container has a hole in the bottom.

- Use potting soil or a seed-starting mix you can buy at the nursery.
- Dampen soil before you fill the container.
- Poke a hole in soil with a chopstick or pencil and add a large seed; for small seeds sprinkle a few on the surface.
- Mist your seeds and keep them in a bright warm place until they start sprouting.

All expert seed sowers caution the following: Don't get fancy; keep it as simple as possible. Buy what you like but don't buy a lot. They also recommend the following thrifty troubleshooting tips to ensure success in growing plants from seed in your garden:

♦ If your soil is full of weeds, prepare the beds by raking them smooth, watering them, and covering them with plastic or row covers. This will warm up the soil quickly, and the weeds will germinate. Cut the weeds down to the ground and, without disturbing the soil, let them grow for another week to ten days. Then start your sowing, again without disturbing the soil. Just water the seeds you sow, not the weeds. When the plants are big enough, you can mulch around the plants and kill off the weeds.

♦ Mix tiny seeds with sand so you know where they are; big seeds will be obvious.

♦ Remember to stand on a board between rows so that you never compact the soil.

♦ Once the seeds show true leaves, start to mulch.

♦ To be really frugal, wait until the seed companies put their seeds on sale in the late summer months. Look for short season varieties (they don't take long to germinate and grow) that will tolerate cool nights and short days; these include beets, kale, carrots, lettuce, mesclun, and spinach.

Germinating Perennial Seeds

Many perennial seeds require a cold treatment to germinate. Doug Green offers the following method as an alternative to the outdoor sowing (outlined above):

1. Take a baggie and fill it with a handful of barely damp vermiculite (a mineral that helps plants grow).

2. Add the seeds you want to germinate to the baggie filled with vermiculite.

3. Write down the name of the seed on a plastic label using waterproof ink. Mark the date.

4. Put the label in the baggie.

5. Seal the baggie and place it in the crisper of the fridge. Let it sit for ninety days.

6. At the ninety-day mark, take the baggie out and sow the seed into a pot of artificial soil and keep it warm on a soil heating mat.

7. When the seedlings get to the four-leaf stage (four true leaves, not seedling leaves), transplant the plants to individual pots and allow them to grow until they are large enough to go into the garden.

Collecting Your Own Seeds

Mary Vinci has been cutting my hair for many years and we've chatted amiably about our gardens, as one does. Mary grows a huge variety of plants on her sunny second-floor deck. She faces west and gets the full blast of the late afternoon sun, so she's set up a barrier against the intense heat since her plants would fry otherwise.

One day I asked her how much she spends on her garden a year. "Oh, last year it was about $10, this year I haven't spent a cent," she replied. Astonished, because I'd seen pictures of her garden, I asked how she could possibly have such a riot of herbs, vegetables, perennials, and annuals for practically nothing. "Most of my plants are from seeds that floated in from the neighbourhood, and some have been given to me by family and friends."

Here are Mary's secrets:

- She isn't fussy about where she finds her containers (corner shops, abandoned on the street) and never buys anything that's not on sale. She has a variety of sizes and stacks them up in different heights to give a sense of being cosseted. One pot turned upside down becomes the base for another.
- Every year she removes the soil from all the pots, mixes it together, and adds fresh compost and topsoil. This way she avoids having any diseases or exhausted soil in any particular pot. The compost is her only expense and she buys it on sale if possible.
- Her best technique is using nothing in her garden that doesn't provide her with viable seeds.

At the exact moment of ripeness, she plucks off the deadheads of her favourite flowers, spreads out the seed and lets them air for a couple of days. Each group of seeds is then put into carefully labelled envelopes. Her criterion is to nurture anything that self-seeds, loves the sun and will flower to produce seeds.

A note on viable seeds: Both annuals and perennials will give up seeds at the end of the season. But cultivars (cultivated varieties) are plants bred for a special reason (colour, longevity, hardiness) and their seeds most likely won't come true — that is, the offspring won't be exactly the same plant the following year. The seed will probably revert to one of the parents, usually the toughest one, and could be quite a different form or colour. So if you collect seeds, stick to species plants, not cultivars.

Here's what Mary grows in her colourful "seedy" jungle:

ANNUALS THAT SELF-SEED:

Name	Number of Years in Mary's Garden
Columbine (*Aquilegia*)	10 years
Spider flower (*Cleome hassleriana*)	10 years
White obedient plant (*Physostegia virginiana*)	15 years, then two pink flowers appeared two years ago
Four o'clocks (*Mirabilis jalapa*)	15 years
Snapdragons (*Antirrhinum majus*)	15 years
Pussy cat tails (*Acalypha* spp.)	10 years

ANNUALS WHOSE SEEDS SHE COLLECTS:

Name	Number of Years in Mary's Garden
Angel's trumpet (*Datura*)	4 years (seeds and flowers are poisonous)
Violets (*Viola* spp.)	15 years
Bachelor's buttons (*Centaurea cyanus*)	3 years
Asters (*Callistephus chinensis*)	15 years
Portulaca, moss rose (*Portulaca grandiflora*)	--

PERENNIALS IN CONTAINERS (MARY LEAVES THEM OUTSIDE):

Name	Number of Years in Mary's Garden
Hyacinth (*Hyacinthus* spp.)	2 years
Lily-of-the-valley (*Convallaria majalis*)	7 years
Lavender (*Lavandula angustifolia*)	3 years
Stonecrops (*Sedum acre* and *S. spectabile*)	7 years

In addition, Mary grows herbs including oregano (*Origanum vulgare*), a perennial; parsley (*Petroselinum crispum*), a biennial; and basil (*Ocimum basilicum*), an annual. She collects seed from the basil and it seems to do very well. It's a perfect companion for her cherry tomatoes, which she also propagates. Here's how she does it:

- Pick a very ripe cherry tomato and break it open with your fingers.
- On a sheet of waxed paper, place all the seeds in a single layer. Allow the seeds to dry overnight.
- With your fingernail, gently pull the seeds off the paper and place them in a container or labelled envelope.
- File the seeds alphabetically in a cool, dry place.

Mary is another gardener inspired by what nature offers her. She may have started out collecting seeds accidentally but it's turned into a pastime, which not only gives her pleasure but also feeds her in every way possible.

Growing Vegetables from Seed

Some people find growing vegetables from seed intimidating. I certainly did when I had my very first garden, but I'd seen my parents do it so I did what they did: I fluffed up the soil really well, created rows to sow the seeds in, stuck twigs in the ground at the end of each row and tied strings between twigs (to attach the seed package to), and had boards to stand on between rows so I wouldn't compact the soil. That much I'd absorbed by osmosis. I knew enough to water regularly, to thin when necessary, and to pull out weeds. We grew our own vegetables long before it was a trend in the city.

Buying plants is expensive. One tomato plant ready to pop into the ground can cost $4, but you can buy twenty tomato seeds for that amount of money. To be absolutely thrifty, form a co-operative. Choose the seeds that will grow well in your neighbourhood, divvy up the cost of seed with friends, and go into production.

Even more interesting is the return of heritage seed-saving. A heritage plant is one that has a long history that can be traced back to its origins. It has not been altered by our modern technology. And if there are variants, they are odd or different because nature intended them to be that way. Until a very few years ago, saving heritage seeds was back there with the dinosaurs. Who needs them when we can get these fancy new hybrids with their guaranteed times for harvest and predictable uniformity? But now people have discovered the flavour and uniqueness of heritage vegetables, and are keen to preserve them for the future.

Sonia Day, author of *Incredible Edibles*, says the best vegetables and herbs to grow from seed are:

- beets
- carrots
- dill
- green beans
- peas
- lettuce
- soybeans
- summer savory
- summer squash
- tomato
- basil

1. Here are Sonia's easy, step-by-step instructions on propagating vegetables by seed:

A SEASON OF MAGICAL SEEDS

Susan Dyer is a superlative gardener with a large city garden, which almost satisfies her plant-aholic nature. She's a committed devotee of seed sowing. A visit to her spring garden is to see pots and pots of seeds germinating; and on a return visit in summer you will see pots and pots of seedlings merrily doing whatever it is they are supposed to do. She shares her passion for propagating.

Seeds show the magic and the mystery of life. You learn to love gardening through seeds, not through the big plant that makes for an instant garden. That's the magnificent thing about seeds — it's about patience.

I buy seeds from many different sources because I like to experiment. I save some seeds — not from plants that will self-sow — and there are some I couldn't do without. I have a special purple-black poppy I have never been able to find again. And zinnias, wonderful zinnias, which you can grow so easily. Then there's the marvellous plant called Kiss-me-over-the-garden-gate (*Polygonum orientale*), which I found at Great Dixter in England and haven't found anywhere else. Nothing is too much trouble for seeds; most of them are really easy. And maybe this year I'll get all the seeds I sow out of their pots into the ground. It's a promise I make every year.

1. Use a sterile soil mix formatted for seed starting.
2. Plant seed in any shallow container, keep mix damp, and cover with plastic wrap (otherwise green fuzz appears on the surface).

3. Water around base of the seed container. Make sure the water is at room temperature; never use icy water.

4. Whether you keep it in sunlight or in a dark place depends on the seed so check the package to make sure.

5. When the first two leaves — the dicotyledons — develop, add a mild solution of a water-soluble, 15-30-15 fertilizer. Within six weeks, you'll have strong, healthy plants ready to put outside.

Everyone loves to have tomato plants and I'm no different. But I've finally given up after planting the usual number of sets every year — I simply don't have enough sun beating down on my garden. Sometimes you need to give in even when the spirit is willing.

PROPAGATING FROM PLANTS

Since there are so many ways of making new plants, it's handy to know what some of the propagation terms mean:

- **Hardwood cuttings:** These are the whole stems from a woody plant, such as a tree or shrub. They are usually taken in late summer, and potted up to grow roots.
- **Softwood cuttings:** Softwood cuttings are the tips of stems that are cut and potted up to form a new root system.
- **Layering:** This occurs when a stem of a woody plant bends to touch the soil and forms new roots. Nicking the bottom of

SEED BANK SOWERS

Kelly Gilliam started her own seed bank in 2009, with just a handful of seed varieties she'd collected herself. Her business grew very quickly as gardeners from around the world heard what she was doing and wanted to donate seeds from their collections. Here is her story.

The whole purpose of starting my own seed bank was to preserve vegetable varieties that are going extinct, document not only their growth but their histories as well, and then to re-offer and spread the seed to as many people as possible to keep the varieties alive. A few varieties that I'm growing this year aren't available anywhere else (I had to request them from the Canadian government-run seed bank). A few are South American tomato varieties: 'El Nano' and 'Platillo', as well as a few Italian and Russian tomatoes that aren't available commercially; and there are three family heirlooms that I'm helping to spread as well: 'Mr. Tung's' and 'Irish Conners' pole beans, as well as 'Slocan' snow peas.

I am always scouting out ways to get seeds for the seed bank, and since I focus on heirloom and OP (open pollinated) veggies, the small selection that you can buy just doesn't satisfy those needs. So for the most part I swap with folks from all over the world. It's cheap, and the best part is you have access to seeds you normally can't buy commercially. Plus you get to talk to people, hear the histories of the varieties (my seed bank rigorously documents these!), and sometimes you hear stories first-hand from the families who've been growing the varieties for a hundred years (or more).

I really like self-sowing annuals (borage being my favourite, though it does reseed prolifically), because they're just so easy. I usually get my perennials from friends who need to divide plants.

As for setting up a network, it's pretty loose: I have a group of people I go to for growers for the seed bank every year, and for the actual swapping I go through Seeds of Diversity; and then mainly it's just the gardening websites and forums with a lot of really active seed swappers.

the stem can encourage rooting. Cover the rooting section with soil and wait until you pull at it and it feels like it's taken hold. Then cut it off from the parent plant, dig it out, and voilà — a new rooted plant.

- **Dividing:** Take any fairly large, extremely healthy plant and whack it in half vertically. (A very large plant can be divided into many pieces, as long as each has some roots.) You can perform this surgery with either a large bread knife, or the sharp part of a garden spade. Or rip it apart with your fingers. You now have two (or more) plants and can put them in the garden or in separate containers. Water slowly and deeply, then top dress by adding some compost all around the new plants.

Let's take one gardener as an example who uses all these methods of adding to her garden. Lorraine Robertson, who gardens in England, is a firm believer in propagation in all its forms:

- If you buy annual geraniums or fuchsias and have no place to save them over winter, take a pot of cuttings (stems you cut off the plant) and keep it on a windowsill; in the spring you can pot up new plants. You must give cuttings a damp atmosphere so cover the pot with a plastic bag until the cuttings are rooted; you'll know they're rooted when you see new growth. You will feel proud of yourself.

+ Learn to take softwood or hardwood cuttings and to layer plants. Then you can buy one plant and have several next year or sooner. My garden is full of shrubs and soft fruit I have grown from cuttings. I brought enough boxwood cuttings from our last garden to make two hedges in the new garden.

+ I hate to throw away prunings so I stick a few in the ground or in a pot. They do not always root, but there is nothing to lose and it costs nothing. When I have extras to give to friends, they in turn will give me cuttings from their plants.

Larry Davidson of Lost Horizons is an inspired plantsman, and his fabulous website, (www.losthorizons.ca), is a magnet for serious gardeners. Here's how he suggests propagating using division:

1. Take a healthy, vigorous plant, usually one gallon in size, and pop it out of the container or dig it out of the garden.
2. Lay it on its side on a bench or work table.
3. Using a sharp knife, cut the plant in half so that the top half includes the foliage and the bottom half contains the lower portion of the roots.
4. Take two one-gallon containers and half-fill them with growing compost.
5. Place each of the two halves of the plant on top, facing upward.
6. The top half of the roots with the foliage will grow downward and fill the pot. The tops of the severed roots should be visible

on top. They can then be lightly covered with compost and kept lightly moist.

7. In a month or two, depending on the species, each root will sprout. At that point they can then be repotted up individually or placed in the garden. This is a quicker method with less disease and rotting because there is less root disturbance. This technique works well with many species, including *Acanthus, Anemone, Crambe, Dicentra, Eryngium, Papavar, Phlox, Primula* and *Verbascum*.

When you go to plant society meetings, always ask the people there for their best propagating tips. You'll be astonished about how ingenious gardeners can be. Nursery people are working with plants all the time and they, too, have amazing ideas.

Thrifty Propagating Tips

Gardeners are always pretty generous with their knowledge. Here are some tips I've picked up over the years from various places, and also from my own experience:

Egg Cartons

♦ Start seeds in cardboard egg cartons. Place the cartons on a pile of newspaper, set in a warm place, and water. The newspapers will get soaked and keep on moistening the air until they, too, are dried out. You won't have to spray the seedlings quite as often.

- Use egg cartons to store seeds. Put seeds immediately into an egg carton (make sure they're well identified) until you can file them more sensibly.
- Cardboard egg cartons with seedlings can be planted straight into the garden where the cartons will eventually compost down.

Aluminum Foil and Pie Plates

- Smooth out used foil wrap and save it to put out in the garden to brighten up dark areas. The foil will reflect the sun back, and since it's been crinkled, it won't burn the area you are reflecting light on.
- Cut out the centre of a pie plate and poke holes in the bottom. Plant a new seedling in the centre to keep out cutworms.

Steven Biggs and Donna Balzer have written an enchanting book called *No Guff Vegetable Gardening*. I like their style and they contributed the following tips:

Shop Where Professionals Shop

In an age when gardening is fashionable, many consumer gardening supplies are ridiculously overpriced. White clover seed for lawns isn't the only example. For the thrifty gardener who uses a lot of pots or trays — or at least shares a case with other thrifty gardeners — it might be worth a trip to a commercial supplier servicing the greenhouse or nursery industry. Likewise with soilless potting mix: A 3.8-cubic-foot (.11-cubic-metre) compressed bale (a standard industry size) yields roughly 5.7 bushels (200 litres) of mix once expanded. (Most bags of mix sold at garden centres contain .3 to .6 bushels/10 to 20 litres of mix.) Aside from the per-litre cost savings, the quality of commercial-grade soilless mix is very often superior.

Try Old-School Seeding

It was April, and my grandfather from Calgary — whose backyard boasted more vegetables than grass in an era when grass reigned supreme — was visiting us in Toronto. We bought a packet of yellow tomato seeds together, but when we returned home we didn't have much in the way of seeding supplies. He fetched a plastic washbasin from the laundry room, added a few handfuls of potting soil, and then casually sprinkled on some seeds, passing me the packet so I could sprinkle on some more. We covered the seeds with a bit of soil and were done, except for a label made from masking tape. For the thrifty gardener, starting seeds indoors does not require expensive supplies.

Skip the Heat Mat

Gardeners often use heat mats (sources of heat placed below the seeds) to speed up germination. Heat mats are expensive so alternatively if you have hot water radiators, you might be able to put the planted seeds atop the radiators.

Growing from seed, learning to divide and layer, and being imaginative in how you fill your garden on the ground or on high is part of the
pleasure of gardening. It's one way to get kids involved because they
really do see the magic of growing something big from something
minuscule. But you can't grow a garden in any old way, shape, or form.
You have to be to make sure that it's healthy and that comes from good
maintenance.

CHAPTER 7

MAINTAINING
THE GARDEN

This is one of the most curious things about making a garden: People will spend a lot of money having a garden installed, they will devote a king's ransom to new plants, but they are reluctant to spend the time and money on maintenance. About 50 percent of having a thrifty garden is looking after it on a regular basis. This doesn't mean sprinkling a bit of water about and plucking a weed or two. You have to have a system that works for you and a method to keep the garden healthy.

A garden neglected will revert to weeds and nature's whims in about two years. The frugal gardener never walks through the garden without a tool in hand (secateurs, scissors, or a trowel), just in case there is something amiss. Tidying as you go is half the fun, in the words of the late renowned *Esquire* editor L. Rust Hills.

WATERING AT GROUND LEVEL

Countless times clients have said to me, "Don't worry, I can look after the watering," when they don't know the first thing about watering. And haven't a clue that it can quickly become boring, especially during heat waves. They will slack off pretty quickly. The first plants to die (and they will) are the most expensive ones; the tough-as-old-boots second-hand plants will survive because they have survived before and will survive again.

When I and my little crew go to a site, we take watering seriously. We always have four pails with us (a couple of the rubbery kind are easy to carry, but anything will do). We keep the hose going and fill each pail and let it sit for at least twenty minutes so all the chemicals evaporate and the water is tepid. Every hole dug is watered very slowly and carefully to make sure the drainage is good. If it isn't, we add sand and compost; if the water runs off too quickly, we add compost and a thick mulch to keep erosion at bay. But usually this is not a problem because we've done the prep on a whole bed before planting (see Chapter 4).

From the biggest tree to the smallest perennial, each plant is watered by hand. This is the best way to water your garden. And there is a reason for this: It means that you can observe how the water is being absorbed by the soil. Never force the soil to take on more water than it can absorb at a given moment. Often we'll build a little dam with compost or mulch so we can hand-direct the water around the plant. It's impossible to get water below the root system using a sprinkler unless it is left on for hours and moved around every forty-five minutes or so. We never use sprinklers for installation and seldom in the first year afterward if we stay on for maintenance.

Observe the garden: Almost anything, such as a big leaf or a small shrub canopy, will cause a rain shadow, and chances are not much is getting to the soil beneath. After a rain, lift up those hosta leaves and have a look — the soil is probably still dead dry. Evergreens are especially vulnerable to drying out. You may wonder why the needles are brown even though you've been sprinkling away. Usually it's because the water isn't getting to the root system, and the gasping roots suck the life out of the plant.

The best way to water is by bucket. That sounds like a lot of work, and it is. But it's the only way of ensuring a garden is properly watered in those critical first few months of life. And how thrifty is that: You and a bucket of water.

The second best way to water is to leave the hose on the ground on a low, slow dribble. You have to keep moving the hose so it waters all around the plant. This might mean leaving it on for about half an hour if it's a large plant.

The third best way is to stand in the garden with a hose and an attachment such as a watering wand that allows you to get in between plants.

WATERING POTTED PLANTS

Juliet Mannock is one of the most inventive gardeners I know. Here's how she waters hanging baskets and any container that she can hump around easily:

For ballast in containers and baskets, Juliet uses a plastic bag filled with vermiculite (the stuff used to lighten up potting soil) or the plastic pods and popcorn used in packing materials.

- Prepare the water in a watering can. Let it get to room temperature before using.
- Choose a shady spot and on a strong table that can take both water and pots without complaint, set up a steamer pan for jars or a kitty-litter tray, and **half-fill** with cold water.
- Place one of the plants into position in the tray.
- Fill the rest of the tray with water, using the watering can, until any bubbling stops.
- Let the pot sit in situ for a minimum of half an hour to an hour, and then heave it out and let it drain on the table.
- Once it's no longer dripping, put the plant back in its usual spot.

It's that simple, she says. "Potted plants or hanging baskets treated this way need watering at the most once every two days even in the hottest, most humid weather. This treatment is foolproof, can be done at whatever speed you fancy, and, wow, what a difference! Best time to water is early to mid-morning or between 4 and 5:30 in the afternoon."

I usually divide my garden into distinct areas, each one intended for a separate watering session. I'll leave a hose on for a good hour and then move it to another spot. I use an old brass nozzle and stick it in a hose guide to keep it trained on one area. (This is lazy but I've found sometimes I just have to give in.)

It's nice to have a routine for watering. I like to do mine in the early morning. But if you can't do it then, make sure you do it in the late afternoon. Don't leave a sprinkler on during the middle of the day. Most of the water will evaporate. That's when you do stealth watering: with a can or bucket for the plants that are absolutely screaming for help. If you notice that plants are wilting in the heat, rush out and give them a good deep drink no matter what time of day it is. The leaves are wilting for a reason: The roots can't get enough water to compensate for all the water lost through the stomata (little pores) in the leaves, a process called transpiration. Here are some more thrifty watering tips:

- Recycle your grey water. If you don't have a dishwasher, throw your used sink water into the border closest to the house, along with extra coffee grounds, which will break down and acidify the soil ever so slightly.
- Reroute your washing machine water into the garden. This is tricky and will take some plumbing but the effects are terrific.
- Have all downspouts rerouted into a rain butt or into the

garden. This means rain comes off the roof into the garden where it will do some good and won't go flowing off unused into the sewer.

Learn to water your garden properly and it will thrive in even extreme weather conditions. Keep in mind that you want to water below the root system and that it takes time to do so.

WATERING ON HIGH

The number of times you'll be trotting outside to water depends on the aspect of your balcony. A south-facing balcony means you will be doing it twice a day, and if you can't handle that much time, it's a good idea to have some sort of easy automated system, especially if you've got a lot of space to deal with.

No matter which way you face, however, watering will be a daily challenge. You'll be able to tell pretty quickly just how much of a rain shadow is cast by the apartment above and how far you can count on rainwater being driven inside the planting area by the wind.

To save a lot of effort, get into a rhythm of watering as you're having a cup of coffee in the morning, and then again with a glass of wine at night. Don't ever water in midday, certainly not so any moisture hits foliage, or you'll have fried plants. Sonia Day, author of *Incredible Edibles*, offers these thrifty tips for watering your balcony garden:

- Watering by hand means you have to allow the tap water to sit for a minimum of twenty minutes to let all the chemicals evaporate and the water has time to rise to room temperature, which is best for the plants. Keep a filled bucket at the ready so it will be easy to scoop out water whenever you need it.
- Make sure you add water slowly until it runs out the bottom of the container. Here's where a moisture meter can come in handy (make sure the tips are clean).
- Use a turkey baster to suck out the water in the saucers under containers (pots sitting in water get waterlogged, and roots will rot).
- If you are going away for any length of time, you can make a primitive self-watering system: Fill a bucket of water. Cut some long strands of thick wool or sisal twine. Put one end into the bucket and the other end into the soil in your containers. This will wick some (but not much) water into the plants.

There are sophisticated versions of this self-watering system available in online catalogues, but the above will work for a small balcony over a hot weekend.

MULCHING AND COMPOSTING

There are two magic bullets in gardening: To mulch is one of them and to compost is the other. Compost is decaying organic matter used to feed the soil. Mulch is any organic material you lay atop the soil and around plants to keep the temperature even and to keep water from flowing away from plants. It helps retain moisture in the soil and slowly breaks down, feeding the roots as it does so. It's the blanket of life for most gardens, especially if you live in hot areas or extremely cold areas, which most of us do in North America. (For Composting see page 181)

Mulching

Mulching is a habit. Even if you only mulch your most precious plant possessions, you'll find they come through the winter in much healthier condition and usually with no damage whatsoever. Mulch slows down frost-heave, which happens when water in the soil expands as it freezes and pushes plants out of the ground. In spring mulch will feed the soil as it composts down. Additionally, weeds have a tough time making their way through a nice, thick mulch, and any that do pop up are easily seen and routed out. In hot, exposed areas, mulch protects the soil and keeps it from being beaten to a pulp by wind and sun, both of which can turn fine soil into sand pretty quickly. For very little effort, mulching gives a garden huge results.

Mulch around vulnerable plants, or do the entire garden once the soil is hard with frost. You will never regret this action. It also makes the garden look really attractive. NEVER use the hideous dyed mulches. They look awful and make no sense whatsoever. Tacky, tacky. I had a client who had filled his garden with the red version of this stuff. I made him gather it all up in bags and put it on the curb. Now he has a lovely dark combo of duck compost and well-composted pine bark. It's a luscious background for splendid plants.

To add lots of nutrients to her mulches, gardener Lorraine Robertson makes high-fibre compost by adding torn-up cardboard and paper to the organic material so the compost will be bulkier with a better balance of ingredients. She never turns her compost but just waits six months for it to be ready. She then adds it to her mulch to make the latter break down even more quickly to feed the plants. Here are her favourite mulches:

- A combo of compost from the garden plus manure and leaves makes a great mulch. Mix it up and spread it around in November.
- A mix of duck compost as a layer over composted pine bark. It's not cheap, but what amazing action in spring when the plants behave as though they are on steroids.
- Hay and straw are perfect mulch for a country garden.

It's hard to emphasize the importance of mulching enough. As well as keeping plants hale and hearty, it will cut down your work in the garden by about three-quarters.

Tips on Mulching

Artists Tom Miller and Louis de Niverville have a huge suburban garden with many raised rose beds. To keep the maintenance to a dull roar, here's what Tom does in autumn: "Our borders have an abundance of golden oregano. I cut it back a bit in the summer, but by autumn it is once again spilling over the edges of the beds. In early December I cut it back again — severely — and use the cuttings to heap around the base of the rose bushes. Then I cover that with a layer of soil. I mulch this late in the year, because any earlier and the squirrels will bury their treasures in the mounds of mulch and flatten them. I learned my lesson when I had to mulch twice one year."

Gardener Nick Palumbo applies mulch once or twice a year, and suggests the following:

- Put down 6 to 9 inches (15 to 22 cm) of the least expensive mulch you can get — usually shredded hardwood. Load up on it when you see tree services grinding wood in your area.
- Water the fresh-looking lumber every day for a week and it will start to break down. This is far cheaper than buying composted wood chips. By buying the fresh wood chips and doing the composting yourself, you'll save about $100 for 8 to 10 cubic yards (6 to 7.6 cubic metres).
- Sprinkle the wood chips with fertilizer, and then buy a few bags of the mulch you really like and put it over the top of the wood chips. This aesthetic top layer will also help the chips break down.
- When wood chips are added to the mulch, it cuts down on the need to water. It's the perfect growing medium and it's cheap.

You will find other mulches that work well, especially in keeping squirrels away: Stones and gravel are extremely efficient and aesthetic. You can also add beach glass and small shells (if you can find enough of either to cover a surface), which will contribute a handsome regional accent to a border.

Composting

Compost is the other magic bullet of gardening. It's comprised of organic material — just about anything except kitchen scraps with protein in them — that's in the process of breaking down. This same process raises the temperature of the material, thereby killing off any weed seeds, unwanted bacteria, and other beasts, and turning it into a material that looks and smells like sweet soil. Compost feeds the billions of living creatures that make up the soil which, in turn, create the nutrients needed for a plant's root system to thrive.

Composting is cheap and easy. The best way to create your own compost is to cordon off a small area of your garden, dig a hole, and throw everything in it. Add a little bit of soil on the top and the scraps will eventually break down. You can make the loveliest loamy soil this way — if you've got enough years and patience to do so. I did this with the back 30 feet (10 m) of the garden. In went all the dead leaves from the garden itself, then we'd dig holes in different areas where we'd dump kitchen scraps along with dead plants, weeds, and the potting soil from containers. We then covered the whole area with leaves gathered from the street in autumn. It didn't look particularly attractive, and it did take about five years to revitalize the whole area, but the soil is fantastic now and easy to maintain.

You can also build a composter with bits and pieces of wood. Four by four by four feet (1.2 by 1.2 by 1.2 m) is the optimum size.

To speed up the heating process and make the compost pile super active (it is heating up and composting down), add layers of green stuff (grass clippings) and brown stuff (leaves) and dampen it down. Then stir it up with a compost fork (this isn't one of the essential tools, but I find it very useful because the tines are quite far apart and even a short person can move it around easily). In a few days, put your hand over the pile to see how hot it is. If it's smelly and cold, add a layer of manure to the top. The heat will kill off weed seeds.

Time for full disclosure here: I know this isn't the best way to compost, but what I really do is throw everything into the bin and turn it over every week or whenever I can get around to it. When it looks like it's almost done, I toss it into a second bin and start all over again.

It's easiest to spread compost around in spring because you aren't dealing with big plants, though it's sensible to do so whenever a plant really needs a boost. Rather than dig the compost into the ground, which is really unnecessary (the worms will see to that), spread it around the plants.

It's fine to spread almost-finished compost around plants in autumn because it will continue to break down, but use only finished compost with new plants.

Hot Composting Tips

Everybody has their own quirky ways of making compost (though it's not quite cocktail party conversation), but as long as organic material is breaking down it's on its way to becoming compost. Here are some excellent composting tips:

- Garden writer Donna Balzer has incredibly fast-draining soil and wants compost in a hurry. To speed up the process, she gets grass clippings from a landscaper who never uses herbicides and adds them to the composter. She also adds fresh horse manure (now that is hot stuff) to reserved bags of fall-collected leaves. After layering they hit 55°C overnight and, within a few weeks, her hot compost is finished.
- Gardener Juliet Mannock says it's way too much trouble turning over compost to hasten the heating process, so she layers, which is her key to success. She adds anything with felty leaves, and lays twigs crosswise to allow air circulation in the pile; then keeps it moist.

Think outside the composter, from using weeds (seedless) in between rows of vegetables to the shredding of your local newspaper. *Anything* organic can become compost. It will break down and feed the soil but it can look pretty terrible. In that case, overlay it with some material that's more aesthetic to be a background for the plants.

DRYPOSTING

Rob Firing is an old friend who has become a keen gardener because his mother is a great gardener. He's invented "dryposting," an innovative alternative to composting. Here, he shares his tips.

DRYPOST (*noun*, derived from "compost"): Organic material gathered over winter months and stored dry inside for the purpose of conditioning soil in the spring.

When I first set about what I call "dryposting," I was motivated by the desire to compost while not wanting to sacrifice space in my small, raccoon-patrolled backyard in Toronto.

I start in October. It can be done year-round but the materials dry out faster in the fall and winter. The point of this exercise is to have organic material to work into the soil in the spring as soon as the ground can be broken, and to be able to store the material inside until that happens. You don't want it to go mouldy or become food for critters. I made a few mistakes the first year, like putting old quinoa seeds in the batch (which grew up everywhere when I mixed the drypost into the soil the next spring), and impatiently storing partially dry ingredients, which grew mouldy.

Here is what my drypost is generally made of:

♦ crushed eggshells
♦ cut-up wine cork (Cut the cork twice lengthwise with a sharp chef's knife, then slice the eighths three or four times across until they are roughly a pearl-sized wedge. The blender, food processor, and coffee grinder don't work very well and use up lots of energy.)

- past due tea, herbs, and spices
- dried coffee grounds
- seeds that are unlikely to grow (like citrus)
- dried avocado rind
- dried citrus rind
- dried flowers
- woody stems of apples, pears, etc.
- root fibres of leeks and spring onions
- garlic and onion papers
- olive pits (salt rinsed off)
- sunflower seed husks
- nutshells (avoid the salted stuff, or else rinse off the salt)

The three key elements are size, moisture, and food value. I cut the bits with scissors or a knife to a size no larger than a necklace pearl. Or I simply crumble the material with my hands. All must be bone-dry before I add them to the batch, and kept in a paper garden-waste bag out of sight in the basement. Leave avocado rind, spent coffee grounds, squeezed-out teabags, and citrus rind (completely clean of fruit mass) out on the counter or windowsill for a day or two before adding to the drypost batch.

If the bits are too large, they don't mix well enough into the soil and they don't disintegrate fast enough. Avoid grains, flour, cornmeal, root vegetables, bread, and dried fruit. It's mostly about wood fibres, dried leaf matter, and low-starch seed mass. The smaller the better, but not dust. Pearl-sized bits hold their structure just long enough to change the consistency of the soil (for the better, especially if you have clay or sand — I have both in different parts of my small yard), and then they disappear, enhancing the soil in other ways.

Results: The soil under my apple tree the first year (pre-drypost) was close to pure lead clay. When it rained too much, the mound would lose structure, disintegrate, flow onto the garden path, and form muddy ponds that hardened into dinner plates. Armed with a full, packed bag of drypost — I was amazed at how much had accumulated — and a small amount of crumbled bark from a fallen willow next door, I broke up the soil under the apple tree down about 12 to 14 inches (30 to 35 cm), and worked in the material with my hands and a spade. What I found a week later was stunning: The soil was a deeper colour and spongy to step on. It fell out of my hands almost like potting soil. Nearly all the drypost material had disappeared. Before that summer only crabgrass and plantain weed (and an unkillable hosta) grew in that soil. Now ferns and trillium flourish, season after season, with no further soil work. I am now looking forward to reconditioning the rest of the nastiest patches of clay in my garden, so I can take advantage of the little space I have.

If you can't wait until compost is completely broken down, don't worry; it can be effective about three-quarters of the way to its final stage: good-looking humus. Just make sure anything that goes into the composter is chopped up quite small.

Material NOT for the compost:

1. Anything containing protein (meat, bones)
2. Kitty litter and dog droppings
3. Ashes from the fireplace (might contain toxic elements)

THRIFTY AMENDMENTS FOR THE SUSTAINABLE GARDEN

The term "sustainable" is one that is batted around a lot. And the goal in gardening is to be sustainable. The sustainable garden means essentially working with nature, and using eco-friendly products in a garden that is pretty much self-sufficient. But if you must, at some point, buy fertilizer, bug killer, compost, potting soil, or other garden products, buy in an intelligent manner. A well-educated gardener is going to automatically be thrifty, so learn the lingo. Right now there are huge surcharges for anything with the word ORGANIC on it. You can't always trust labels so read them carefully. Here are some useful definitions:

- **Certified Organic:** This is material, seeds, and so on that have been chemical-free for at least five years. It comes with a certification logo.
- **Organic or "Derived From" Organic Products:** Requires only 15 percent organic material and the other 85 percent can be full of chemicals.
- **All Natural:** "All Natural" does not mean the material (compost, topsoil) has not been treated with chemicals. Read the very fine print.

Be especially careful of any bagged product that does *not* tell you what's inside. Someone's "magic compost" might be full of peat moss. And if you don't like peat moss, you'll be paying a premium for it. I was merrily using what I thought was mushroom compost (normally a pretty good product) until I noticed it said, "Mushroom Compost Plus." There's nothing on the label to say what that "plus" is, but it's probably peat moss because it says, "Helps hold water in the soil." Well, that's what compost does anyway. Why pay more for something that should be relatively inexpensive?

To create a sustainable garden means you want it to get along with as little outside intervention as possible. The sustainable garden is full of inventive solutions; here are some of them:

Plastic Bottles

We hate plastic, but it's going to be with us for a long time. So think up some good ways to reuse plastic bottles in the garden, such as the following:

- Poke small holes in the bottom and sides of the big bottles that Epsom salts come in. Bury it up to the neck in an area that's hard to reach or impossible to water. Fill the bottle full of water, and it will slowly and discreetly disperse water to the roots of the plants.
- Cut off the bottom of a long-necked plastic bottle and stick it in the soil. Place it next to a needy plant and regularly fill it full of water.
- Use plastic bottles for containers. They don't take up much space and, with some drainage holes in the bottom, they make a cheap alternative to clay. Plant just like any other container.

Epsom Salts

Sprinkle a generous handful of Epsom salts around roses. This boost of magnesium encourages lush foliage and more stems. However, if you have too much magnesium in the soil already, Epsom salts could make things worse. Before you use them, buy an inexpensive soil test kit and follow the instructions so you don't upset the balance of nutrients in the soil.

Old Pillowcases

Get into the habit of making manure or compost tea. Compost tea is a fast way of getting a wide spectrum of nutrients to the plants, and particularly useful in areas with gravel mulch where you can't add straight compost. You can pour the tea over the stones and know it's going to get into the soil and do its magic. To make compost tea:

- Hang an old pillowcase filled with several cups of manure (or compost) in a covered tub, large pail, or water butt.
- Let it steep for a few days and then remove the leftovers to the compost.
- Drain the "compost tea" from the tub.
- Dilute it two parts water to one part tea (but test this by putting a little around a plant and check to make sure it's okay). Or make a foliar spray with 1 tbsp (15 mL) of tea in four quarts (3.8 litres) of water.

Hoses

Once again we come back to these indispensable items. You can occasionally find abandoned old ones so go on the prowl for them. Here are just a few more uses for them:

- Cut an old hose into easy-to-use lengths (12 inches/30 cm or so) and set them out at night. They will attract slugs and earwigs. Just bang the varmints into a bucket of oily water in the morning.
- Puncture little holes through an old hose. Put it in a difficult-to-reach area and use it as a soaker hose. Attach the new hose to it and turn the water on slowly for an hour or so to really give the surrounding area a good soak.
- Paint an old hose to look like a snake. It might discourage a few marauders, and it will give a little kid a healthy frisson. Move your "snakes" around the garden.

Newspapers

Letting newspapers pile up can be a major thrifty move. First there is the sheer pleasure of reading them, and then look at all of the ways they can be repurposed:

- Shred old newspapers and then toss them into the compost. Put a nice thick layer of soil over them and they will break down quickly. You can do this all winter. Just keep a bag of soil in a place where it won't get frozen or you'll be whacking away at an ice pack.

◆ Extend a border or remove grass by making a pile of newspapers several inches thick over the desired area. Spread a layer of soil over the top of the dampened newspapers. The newspapers will kill off grass and weeds, but they also break down conveniently into compost. You need to do this for at least a season to see results. I saw it done for the first time thirty years ago, and it's still one of the best recycling techniques ever invented.

◆ If you have a persistent invader such as goutweed (*Aegopodium podagraria*), place a layer of dark plastic on top of the area you want to clear. In a couple of weeks, check for any sprouts coming out of the soil and cut them back so they are even with the surface. Pile newspapers on top and then cover it all with compost.

◆ When you are prepping containers, instead of lining them with Styrofoam, use thick layers of newspapers. This won't get them through the coldest weather but it means you can water less often.

◆ Buy a little wooden form called a Potmaker, and shape your own pots out the newspapers. Perfect for seedlings. The pots naturally decompose in the ground, so seedlings can be planted pot and all.

Vinyl Blinds

Who would have thought anyone would finally get rid of vinyl blinds? But eventually some of them wear out and they can still be put to use:

- Chop up the blind sections and write down plant names in pen, or paste plant IDs on them. Include common, botanical names, plus light and water requirements.
- Stick vinyl blind sections straight into the garden to indicate what's been planted. (Though I must say it's not a great look.) Use them to mark an area where you've planted bulbs. They're easy to remove and a good way to announce what'll come up in spring.

GOOD GARDENING MAINTENANCE HABITS

A lot of gardening really has to do with rituals and habits. If you start out with charming rituals (such as watering with a glass of wine in your hand) or good garden habits right from the very beginning of your gardening life, you'll find an even more profound level of pleasure. Good grooming goes a long way in the garden, and it shouldn't take a lot of time or aggravation. And a big part of "grooming" includes making sure to keep all of your tools and gardening essentials organized. Here are some tips for getting into good gardening habits:

- Put your tools away immediately. It's so easy to leave things lying around when you are exhausted at the end of the day.

Keep pails or boxes in strategic places in the garden and dump stuff into them as you go by. Then you've only got three things to pick up before you get to that glass of wine. I learned this from clutterbuster Kate Seaver (see also page 228).

♦ Apply indoor principles to outdoor organizing: Ten minutes a day just tidying up, picking up, and looking at what could be made more efficient. I no longer have the energy to clean up giant messes, but little messes are a good deal less daunting.

♦ Never buy things you can't use outside all year round. Pay more money and get good stuff. Why use up the time and energy and space on something that's cheap and has to be looked after?

♦ Keep track of unnecessary duplicates. There's always someone out there who needs it more than you do. This is especially true with school and community gardens where more tools are always welcome.

Never let gardening become a burden. You want a garden to be something you are proud of and good habits create good gardens.

There are some profound rules that go with gardening and one is never to neglect it. An untended garden can turn into a haven for weeds in a matter of months. And, once out of control, it is that much harder to get back into shape. Developing good habits, no matter how unimportant they seem in the beginning, is a long way on the road to thrifty gardening. Never allow yourself to get discouraged since you want to be able to see the garden with a good deal of clarity so you can get to the next stage — decorating the garden. Garden décor is one of the most charming and some of the best fun you can have. It's not just another black hole for money. It's making your gardening life even more creative.

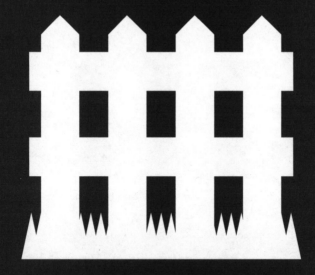

CHAPTER 8

DECORATING
THE GARDEN

You can't decorate your way to a great garden, but you can make a very ordinary place into something quite special with the right details. Decorating the garden is the icing on the cake. You can eat the cake with pleasure, but think of how much more delicious it is with icing. So it is with garden décor — an unadorned garden is still a garden, but there's something about the addition of personal fillips that makes a handsome garden look even better.

Garden furniture can be expensive if you buy the well-designed, high-end stuff. Therefore, consider purchasing furnishings very carefully. It can be a statement, a pleasure, and a thing of beauty. Buy one good piece of garden furniture and get the rest of the stuff on the street or out in the wilds, and you are on your way to developing a garden style. I bought some wonderful chairs for our deck. They are so well-made that thirty years later we still use them every day in our garden dining room. The deck and the table have gone through drastic changes but these chairs are for life.

Of course, to be frugal you always start with the simplest move possible. An elegant and easy way to make your garden look like it's custom-designed is to echo some of the colours of the house in important garden structures: If you love the trim colour, for instance, carry it into the garden by painting the fence the same colour.

It's also important to make sure you have winter interest. Evergreens of course do a magnificent job, as do many ornamental grasses. But a piece of well-placed furniture or a sculptural object — a bench, a big marble bowling ball — can hold snow and be a calm and elegant moment in the winter garden. This is the season when carefully selected rocks will add a huge amount of drama to the garden.

Many years ago, I started decorating my deck and now have strong evidence (embarrassing photographs) that less is definitely more. I added and added: Furniture from the Salvation Army; discarded wicker; a pew from an abandoned church; mirrors on either end of the deck; a dozen different sizes and styles of pots. Nothing escaped my grasping hand. It began to resemble a tatty second-hand store. Once the deck was full, extra bits and bobs spread out into each border.

Eventually, I felt my garden was chattering at me, there was so much stuff lying about. Then one day a basic element of style hit like an epiphany: Remove one-third of existing tchotchkes and everything will quiet down. I set to work immediately and had a major yard sale.

Though I still have dozens of *objets trouvés* nestling in the garden, they are hidden by vines and mature plants and always give a little frisson of pleasure when I uncover them. Over all these decades, I have bought very few expensive pieces for the garden. One exception being a magnificent sculpture fountain by Reinhard Reitzenstein, who is a wonderful artist. It's perfectly placed to be the central focus from the dining room to the most immediate part of the garden. The sound is blissful and it looks glorious bedecked with snow.

Before you get to the decorating stage, fluff the garden to the level of neatness you want to maintain. The tidy garden will always be a satisfying garden even when you are broke — especially when you are broke. Then start adding those beautiful elements that will make your garden intimate and personal.

DECORATING THE GARDEN ON THE GROUND

Decorating a garden is as complex and layered as decorating a room in the house. You have to have a colour scheme, a sense of style to aim for, and a budget. Invest in good furniture or refurbish fine old furniture. Don't just throw stuff at the garden because it's cheap or it's on sale. Each item should be considered very carefully. Keep simplicity in mind. The less cluttered your garden is, the easier it is to handle.

Overdoing the details will mess up your head as well as your eyes. If your garden can't hold the amount of stuff you want to stick outside, have a sale.

Organize areas into work, play, and entertaining. Then go at decorating each section, keeping in mind that you are working towards an overall style. It's even nicer when you've got a focal point or centrepiece for each area that gives you some kind of visual pleasure: The perfect chair to rest under a tree; a little greensward for kids to play on; an attractive potting shed. But most of us don't have the time or money for all of these items. So pick one and concentrate on making it the best you can.

There are kits you can put together to make a garden shed (or gazebo or pergola). But finding pieces of old wood fashioned together to make an outside storage area can also have its own charm. A lean-to or a table can work just as well, as long as you have some place to do the dirty work.

Putting a work of art in the garden, whether it's a rock you particularly like or a piece of fine art, is tricky business. Get it wrong and it will drive you nuts. Any work of art, fine or otherwise, is a demanding presence that can move the eye up or down. But it will inevitably draw attention to itself, so be very conservative about dotting the landscape with both art and junque. Placement is very much like planting a large shrub. Here are some tips on placement:

♦ Know which side the piece will be viewed from. Does it have a best side — a face?

- The base of the object is critical, especially if it's a found object. The base will be its anchor, and if it looks unstable or just plain ratty, it will ruin the whole effect. A coat of paint will disguise all manner of flaws.
- If you have a figure, install it at eye level to make a strong psychological impact.

Don't underestimate how important garden décor can be in creating a more finished look to any style of garden. Every single item you put into the garden should count on several levels: Aesthetics, fulfilling a role in a layer of the garden (the statue of a beautiful girl should probably be at eye height, rather than loom over the viewer in a frightening way). Every aspect of furnishing the garden should be fun, but it shouldn't be frivolous. Hold those abandoned toilets.

Waterworks

Every garden needs some form of water. A murmuring water feature not only provides clean water for birds and insects but also helps to block out persistent, throbbing city noise. Here are a few thrifty suggestions for setting up waterworks in your garden:

- Buy an inexpensive circulating pump, let it sit in a lovely old vase or wide-lipped pottery container, and you will have the least expensive fountain possible. Set the container on a patio stone (of course near an electric outlet) and you're set to turn it on.

SERENDIPITY IN THE COUNTRY GARDEN

Susan Harriell lives in the country, thriving almost off the grid, and is a constant finder of the unusual. She wanted structures in her garden and here's how she started out:

Several years ago I saw an old three-sided TV antenna tower sitting at the end of a driveway, waiting for garbage day. I pulled it apart into three sections and took it home. I knew that one day I would have a place for it. As part of my garden creation/renovations, I made a bed in the sun for butterflies. The tops of two of the antenna pieces were bent to mimic the crown of the former top section. I found a fellow to dig 4-foot (1.2-m) holes and set the three pieces in concrete at the back of the new bed. Due to the steep hill and their decreasing heights, the pieces stand symmetrically "stepped" a few feet apart down the hill. They are also covered with vines and much visited by butterflies.

♦ Get a kid's pool, paint it an amazing colour, and set it in the ground by preparing a hole to the exact size. Add some sand for ballast, maybe a rock or two, and a submersible circulating or fountain pump. What you plant around the pond will make it dazzling. This is the place to put those broken bits of statuary, at least one plant with big leaves such as rodgersia (*Rodgersia* spp.) as a focal point, and a complementary tapestry of plants.

♦ Nick Palumbo is one of the most sensible professional gardeners I know and he always finds a way to use water in his clients' gardens. In one garden, he was stuck with a really ugly lilac. He cleaned it out, leaving three of the most attractive branches to keep on growing. At the base he put pea gravel with an edging made of stone rescued from a hotel demolition. "These are stones with a history," he says. "New rocks from a quarry don't have the patina or erosion of these old ballast rocks found under our old buildings." The lilac turned from being an eyesore to the focal point along the fence. To complement it, he built a waterfall out of old Wiarton stones. The water splashes into a preformed pond, which he considers to be much sturdier than the traditional liner-and-sand construction and a lot easier to maintain.

♦ Another Nick trick is to create a swamp or bog garden with a little wooden bridge over it connecting the front and back gardens. A preformed plastic pond without any holes in it is set into the ground, then filled with plants that love to have wet feet.

One word of caution: Animals love to muck around in newly planted little goodies near water. Whether they are hungry or not, they will be curious. Protect the pond with a net covering until the plants have time to get established.

Mirrors and Windows

Mirrors are a clever way of making a garden feel much larger. One of

THE THROWAWAY GARDEN

Valerie Murray's astonishing garden is filled with subtle decorative elements that never scream for attention. She has wonderful *objets* scattered about in what seems to be a casual way though it's anything but. Each piece is discovered with affection and placed with great care. Something you'd never suspect would work outside is both ornamental and adds a delicious element of surprise — for example, a handsome old vase adds an unexpected grace note when set among her plants. She moves things constantly and just as constantly she looks in odd places for the right things to enhance the look of the garden and add to its furnishings:

"Though it's always hard to find items to blend in, I've found throwaways work well. I wanted a solid granite column for the front garden. But it was way too expensive so I went to the local dump and found a great piece of sewer pipe about 10 inches (25 cm) wide and 4.5 feet (1.4-m) high that a workman had just deposited. He offered to drop it off at the house the next time he went by. Then I went to the place where they do graveyard stonework and bought a piece of finished granite for the top. It looks perfect.

"The municipality was getting rid of metal catchment strainers. About 16 inches (40 cm) across, with handles, they are used to stop leaves from getting into the sewers. Because they are full of holes, they make terrific planters, and their grey colour makes them practically invisible in the garden."

Not everyone has as discerning an eye as Valerie, but it's something you can train yourself into. For instance, if you look at paintings long enough, you begin to understand what they mean, how they work and to be moved by them. Well, the detritus of other people's lives can be the same. You have to see into what's discarded and perceive new ways of using things. What we think of as everyday, perhaps even banal, objects can work extraordinarily well in the garden.

my best garden finds was a large, bevelled-edge mirror with a mouldy frame. We rescued it from the garbage and stripped it of the frame. For many years, it leaned against a fence with plants growing up around it, almost obscuring it. When I actually had some money and hired landscape architects to add structures to the garden, they included two real mirrors in their design. I love it. But one thing you must be aware of: Birds might attack their own reflections as interlopers. Let silver foil strings hang down to break up the image.

- If you have a narrow garden, put a mirror on an angle to make it seem much wider.
- You can find inexpensive mirrors in dollar stores. A bright coat of paint will improve a boring frame.
- Add mirrored panels to an abandoned window frame. You can peel and paste them into the glass part and use the frame in the garden.
- Knock the glass out of an old window frame; put it up as a screen; and grow vines across, behind, or over it. Put several together and place them in a zigzag shape for stability.
- Put an old horizontal window frame above a fence to give a bit of height without offending neighbours.
- Hang windows on fences, peeling paint and all, or cut a hole in a fence and insert an old window frame to let light and air through. This also works really well on decks.
- An old window can make the ideal lid for a raised bed to grow

seeds in the early spring. Buy the box-like forms or knock them together out of bits of wood made to match the size of the window. Add a prop so you can leave the lid open when it gets too warm. And make sure it's facing where the sun will hit in early spring. You want the seeds to start germinating as early as possible.

Keep training your eye to pick up what's good and what looks like a nice fit in your garden. Take the same eye out to strange places — dump sites and recycling bins — and see what you might spot that will enhance the garden without looking tacky or cheap. Something well-made or with good form goes a long way in garden décor.

Trellises

Trellises can make a compelling visual impression by creating a strong horizon line or contrasting vertical lines. There are various styles of *treillage* and most recently horizontal slats have been used to create a very modern look. Lattice composed of large (4-inch/10 cm) squares is also a good contemporary look. The prefab crisscross trellis you can buy cheaply can be used in various ways as long as it's well disguised. The look you want is custom-made. Whatever type of trellis you use, it should have enough transparency to let passing breezes blow through.

Lorraine Robertson is a very thrifty gardener, and here are a couple of her tips:

- Use a trellis to improve an unattractive fence, screen an undesirable view, and add privacy.
- Grow annual climbers against a trellis. If you make the trellis detachable and store it in a dry place for the winter, it lasts much longer.

Have a look at different types of material for your trellis. For example:

- Bamboo canes are really good-looking and can be nailed or lashed together to create a trellis-cum-screen.
- Hardware cloth is metal sheeting that comes in rolls. The one with wide (2-inch/5-cm) openings makes a very handsome trellis.
- Fishing line is my favourite way to make a trellis. Get very heavy strong line. It's transparent and you can twist it around nails and make an almost invisible support for vines.

Always install a trellis so that there is a space of about 1 inch (2.5 cm) between the wall it's against and the trellis itself. This will allow air to circulate behind the plant.

Rocks

We love rocks, but we abuse, unforgivably, what is a non-renewable resource. Huge rocks are too often hauled into little bitty gardens and plunked thoughtlessly into place by a machine. Apart from being unique, a rock is a thing of beauty when positioned properly. A small garden needs just one major rock to be transformed. A single stone can act as a sentinel presiding over the garden; several stones can anchor plantings, define edges, or be turned into fountains. Gardener Nick Palumbo says, "Rocks may be expensive, but once you plant a rock, when do you ever have to plant it again?" What could be a thriftier investment?

But a rock is going to cost. It's the weight. Transportation is what makes up most of the cost of big, landscaper-type rocks. It's possible to find terrific rocks piled up on country properties (usually farms), but you must get permission to remove them and lugging them home is a big job. Here's a thought: If you can find a cache of them and someone who's willing to let them go for almost nothing, get a group together and hire a heavy truck and the means of getting the rocks on and off the truck bed.

Here are some of Nick's tips:

- Stones or beach rocks make a good-looking mulch, helping to keep weeds down and holding moisture in the soil.
- In summer and fall, rocks should be like a human body — subtly clothed; that is, surrounded by plants. In winter, you need to see them for their inherent character.

- A rock will serve as a picture frame for the plants surrounding it. If you have a small rock, place it on a few bricks instead of burying it in the soil. Then bring the soil up and around the bricks and the bottom of the rock. Plant very closely.
- Find broken statues and containers, and place them around a rock in a decorative way, giving the impression of crumbling into eternity.
- Go to the manufacturer directly and buy flawed rocks with holes already drilled in them. Plant them with sedums that will grow through the holes.
- Put a rock on a pedestal, and the garden will acquire a sense of solidity and a feeling of great age.

Rocks can define the shape of a garden, add depth to a design, or be a focal point. They should never be dotted about casually or just dumped. They have character and form, which should be respected. The Japanese understand this intimately, and much is to be learned from studying photographs of their gardens and seeing how creatively rocks can be used.

Garden Lighting

Cheryl Moss is a thrifty gardener who loves to change the look of her garden with every season. Here are her fantastic frugal recommendations for lighting the garden:

- I have a pond off the patio and wanted some form of candle-holders. One year I bought a dozen metal shepherds' hooks 4 feet (1.2 m) tall for a dollar each. At the dollar store I picked up a few 6-inch (15-cm) metal birdcages and painted them matte black. I stuck a few of the hooks around the pond and hung the cages from them. On still evenings, I put a tea light in each one for a wonderful glow over the water.

- I wanted orbs floating in the pond and tried glass ones but they were much too fragile and shattered. One year I bought gold and silver plastic Christmas balls of all sizes on sale. Next spring I tossed them into the pond and am so pleased with the look — like giant bubbles.

- I enjoy dining outside by candlelight and love chandeliers. So I visited the dollar store, bought a six-light unwired one, and hung it over the patio table. When there's a party, I light candles in it and the effect is amazing! All for 20 bucks.

Every garden needs thoughtful lighting. An overlit garden is just as uncomfortable as an underlit one. You can use lighting in mysterious and, yes, magical ways. You don't need much: A light up a tree, along a pergola, or emphasizing a favourite plant. We have too many long nights in our country not to have good lighting.

Summer Sails

Cheryl Moss has also come up with an ingenious way of creating thrifty shading for her outdoor patio garden. Here's what she did using her pergola and some inexpensive drapery:

- Get about 14 yards (12.8 m) of sheer drapery fabric.
- Measure, cut, and sew five panels each, 14 feet (4.2 m) long by 2 feet (60 cm) wide.
- Sew plastic drapery rings every 3 feet (90 cm) or so in the drapery panels, and drill tiny holes in the beams of the pergola about 2 feet (60 cm) apart.
- Lace thin wire through the holes and the rings, then twist to fasten them together.

The total cost for Cheryl's DIY shading was about $90. The sheer drapes cut the rays yet let in light, and rain goes right through them. There's a lot of ease to the fabric so when the breeze picks them up, they don't strain and tear. Once the leaves start to fall, they are taken down and stored for the next year.

DECORATING THE THRIFTY BALCONY

One sound principle of all decorating is to buy the highest quality furniture you can possibly afford. It is even more important for balconies because they are quite literally in your face. Good furniture will look smart all year round, and you won't have the horrendous

A MEMORABLE GARDEN

Andrew Larsen, author of The Imaginary Garden *and other children's books, knows that the love of nature has very deep roots. Here's his story.*

A few years ago my mom moved from our old house to an apartment. Like many people her age, moving into an apartment was a small part of a much larger change. Some aspects of the change were exciting. Some were sad. The loss of her garden was tragic.

Her apartment has a north-facing balcony. It's windy and loud, looking out over a busy highway. For the first month or so, my mom would sit on the balcony with a cup of tea, close her eyes, and try to imagine the sounds of birds and the smell of flowers. She would try to imagine that her concrete balcony was a garden.

As that first spring warmed into summer she decided to make her imaginary garden real. She bought some artificial grass and laid it out on the balcony floor. She filled the balcony with spider plants, hoping they could survive its harsh conditions. They did — brilliantly! She put an old rocking chair out there. The next year she brought out some philodendrons and got an assortment of annuals. She began collecting garden sculptures. She even installed a fountain so she could hear the sounds of a falling brook. Her balcony slowly became an oasis, fourteen floors up.

Years have passed. My mom still cherishes her balcony, and spring still holds the same sort of promise as it does for earthbound gardeners. She has a large collection of plants that winter indoors. Some have been nurtured from clippings given to her by friends. They have grown as strong as the very friendships they symbolize. And every year just after the May 24 weekend, my mom faithfully hauls her collection of plants outside. When she's done arranging them, she sits in her rocking chair with a cup of tea, opens her gardening books, and dreams of the season ahead.

task of lugging stuff up and down to storage. Observe the old frugal adage: *Buy well and you buy once.* This is true investment shopping, and the sales make it worthwhile to wait even if it's for a year or two or three.

Sander Freedman is a landscape architect with a special talent for designing Zen-like balcony gardens. He says, "Indoor-outdoor connections in new condos with floor-to-ceiling windows is critical to enhance any lifestyle as well as extend the space, especially in small condos." He suggests the following:

- Break up the box-like feeling of a balcony by clustering pots in groups that follow the balcony edge, but position them in a slightly irregular fashion and lay river rock around the pots. This easily gives ground plane interest at low cost. Make sure the pots are set to keep the rocks from rolling and falling if there's open space between the bottom of the rail and the balcony floor.
- Carry interior colours outside in accent pillows, floor mats, umbrellas, or even dinner mats on the table.
- Make sure that any fabric you use outside is weather resistant (Sunbrella is a good product).
- Consider placing furniture on the diagonal in a corner to kill the right angles and break the box-like linearity of most balconies. You can also use upright urns with cascading flowers or a clutch of bamboo poles.

Many designers hate balcony gardening because you never know what kinds of problems — from a deep rain shadow to relentless wind — may be involved. These suggestions will start you on the road to having a lovely garden no matter where you are.

Flooring

You can't ignore something as raw as the concrete base most balcony or terrace gardens have. Here are some ways to make them softer and more inviting:

- Use inexpensive straw mats from Chinatown to cover the floor. They are relatively cheap and could be replaced anew each year if they get too dirty.
- Get different (harmonious or contrasting) carpets for each area: A seating area one colour, a dining area another, lounging yet another. You can find extremely attractive, inexpensive rugs in most big-box stores. They are weatherproof so you need only to rinse them off or sweep them occasionally. They come in almost every size from 2 by 3 feet (60 by 90 cm) to 9 by 12 feet (2.7 to 3.6 m).
- There are attractive fabric rugs that can be tossed into the laundry on a regular basis.
- Oriental rugs were originally intended to be used in heavy traffic in the middle of the desert, so why not on a balcony? Find a good rug merchant who can give you all the details.

One caution: If you have direct sun, it will fade the most expensive of carpets (inside or out).

♦ Wood tiles are an easy way to cover institutional-looking concrete tiles or concrete slab floors.

Check out second-hand stores and online sites that sell home furnishings. You never know when you'll turn up a small treasure that will work on a balcony floor.

Screens

Solid or see-through, screens can save a balcony design (just as they do on the ground) by defining the space, dividing it into rooms, concealing one part from another (your work area from your sitting area, for instance), improving privacy, or simply adding a decorative element. On the functional side, screens can provide shade, reduce the impact of wind, and support plants.

♦ Shoji screens can divide even a small space and make it look mysterious.

♦ Buy inexpensive lattice and paint it a rich, glowing colour such as eggplant. It will enhance just about any plant you let run over it.

♦ Old wicker ware is amazingly versatile. Check out garbage day and yard sales to find bits and pieces you can tie together to make a reliable windbreak. For a quick paint job, take it to a garage where they spray paint cars and have it sprayed. Otherwise, paint over it by hand and fill in the finicky spots with a spray can of the same colour.

♦ Bamboo is attractive, light, and remarkably versatile. It comes in sheets or rolls, is easy to attach to concrete or wood and makes a solid wall against the prevailing wind.

♦ Look for metal gates, railing, and anything ornamental that can be attached to a concrete or wooden backdrop. It makes a sturdy wall trellis for vines and also acts as a windbreak.

♦ Umbrellas are ideal for providing a ceiling (and some shade) to an outdoor space. If there is little room, small or half-circle umbrellas are now available.

♦ Building screens into the backs of planters can help to define an outdoor area, increase privacy, and also create a pleasing backdrop for plants. Screens secured to solid weighted objects in this way can better withstand exposed wind conditions. Ensure the screens are not higher than the screens installed by the builder between you and your neighbour, or seek permission from the neighbour, management, or board if you want them higher.

♦ If you have a Juliet balcony, hang pots of plants from it to make a screen from the outside world.

The point of all good garden design is to provide a feeling of being cosseted, and working with a balcony garden is no different. You'll enjoy it a lot more if you feel as though you are sitting in your protected little "cave," looking out into the world. It's a sense of security built into our DNA from the time we really did live in caves!

Containers

Cheryl Moss is one of the thriftiest but most stylish gardeners I know. When she got sick of all of her plastic containers, she decided to personalize them. Here's how: "Gently sand the area you want to paint, it doesn't take much; then stencil a design. I've used everyday craft acrylics and coated them with a couple of layers of shellac. The planters treated this way have withstood all seasons without a chip."

You can buy cheap plant holders (urns, window boxes, containers of every size) and custom design them for very little money.

Or enlist a kid: Buy some tubes of craft paint and make painting the pots into a game. Kids will come up with extraordinary designs and colour combinations.

I once interviewed an amazing rooftop gardener who took all the shells he'd collected from his travels around the world and glued them onto cheap terracotta pots and waste-paper baskets he bought from a dollar store. With a few holes punched in the bottom of the latter, he had a perfect planting pot. The look on his terrace was consistent and reflected his personality. The shells were lots of work and lots of fun; however, you can't leave pots like this out to freeze and thaw. Be prepared to store them if you don't live in a warm winter climate.

To give terracotta pots a beautifully aged look, try the following:

CREATIVE PAINTING

John Statham is proprietor of an exciting nursery called John's Garden Centre, which is filled with amazing conifers and perennials, and he likes to have fun with the way he uses plants to decorate the garden.

One year, when I knew the local horticultural society was visiting the garden, I refolded a box around the spent blooms of my large alliums, then painted them red, blue, and white. The painted flowers lasted for about a month. It was great fun watching people run up to these large bright red flowers in my garden, trying to figure out what they were.

I did the same thing to my hydrangea tree one year as part of my Christmas decorating.

I've used floral paint on frozen flowering cabbages as part of our Christmas/winter containers.

When I need to use stakes, I use the dyed bamboo from my Christmas containers. I did up a tomato and Swiss chard container one year, and used thick red bamboo and lime green wire to support the tomato plant.

An upright juniper went into decline but the birds liked it so I cut off all the branches about a foot (30 cm) from the trunk and planted annual and tropical vines at the base. They filled almost every inch of it, and it looks columnar from a distance but is covered in a variety of flowers when you get closer.

- Rinse out your yogurt containers with water and saturate the pots with it, or paint plain yogurt onto a presoaked pot.
- With an old rag, brush wood stain on the pots, clean off any

excess, and let dry. Add as many layers as possible to get a very sophisticated look to the depth of tone.

- Using a sponge, apply old-fashioned, biodegradable milk paint to the terracotta surface. There are dozens of lovely paint colours to choose from and you can make your container collection look consistent, which is important in a confined space like a balcony.

- Take a handful of moss spores and 2 cups (500 mL) each of buttermilk and beer with a sprinkle of sugar. Mix together in a food processor, then paint the goop on the pots. Keep them moist with a mister and watch them evolve into ancient mossy artifacts.

Containers are going to be the main element in your balcony garden design. Make sure they are in good condition; anything chipped and marred will be an eyesore instead of a subtle background for plants.

Decorating isn't the final step to having a wonderful garden, but it usually comes last on the list because it's not something you do all at once. It evolves as you collect pottery, art, and furnishings, and as you develop your own personal style. So never ignore scavenging finds, pickups on recycling day, and those giddy moments of serendipity uncovering a piece you must have. Nothing looks foolish in the garden if you love it.

CHAPTER 9

DOWNSIZING AND SELLING
THE GARDEN

The final chapters of a book are a bit like the final chapters of a gardener's life. You start thinking about all the things you've learned, and what you have learned to do with and without. Doing without is now called "downsizing" and it's a complex idea. It can mean you've lost your job, or you have to change the size and breadth of your life, or you must sell the house and therefore the garden.

How much time you have to devote to the garden is something you should be aware of from the beginning. So many of the gardens I see are a mess because the owners just don't have enough time to take care of their size and scale. So part of downsizing is learning to adjust our ideas about gardening to the space we've been allotted. The longer you garden the more difficult it can be physically and the wilier you become in how you use your energy. Gardening should never be a tedious chore. The minute it does become one, it's time to start imagining ways to make it simpler, more in line with what you are capable of doing.

Then there's the age factor. We hate to admit we aren't as energetic as we were at forty or even fifty, let alone at twenty or thirty, but to recognize your limits can be a source of strength. Give in, admit you can't lug around sacks of compost, haul shrubs out of the ground, and spend ten-hour days planting during the spring and autumn. It's facing up to the loss of being able to *do it all* that is extremely difficult, not the actual chores. Attitude is a huge part of gardening.

DOWNSIZING TO A THRIFTIER GARDEN SPACE

There comes a time in your life when you start to figure out better methods to garden that will match your own energy. One of the ways I've chosen is to add more evergreens to my design. Hardly radical, you think. But way too often these plants are mere afterthoughts and seemed to be so in my garden. They were used strictly to add punctuation to borders and, of course, winter animation.

My strategy on evergreens emerged a few years ago. Every time a perennial croaked or I decided to move it elsewhere, I replaced it with an exquisite little evergreen. As always, I have an annual budget and these are my splurges. They are worth every penny as they are happily companionable with Japanese maples, grasses, and dogwoods — the other plants that do so well in this area. The mix is really glorious because the plants complement each other, they look good all year round, and about the only thing I have to do is the odd bit of tidying up.

Grasses are another good gap filler. They require almost no care except for a whacking back in the spring and they give good year-round value. I'm especially fond of Japanese forest grass (the all-yellow *Hakonechloa macra* 'All Gold' is fabulous). It looks okay in winter with its soft faded brown silk effect, and when whacked back the minute it shows new tips in spring, it grows in the most sensual way. If it starts to looks ratty, I just cut it back. The very first Japanese forest grass plant I bought years ago has been divided and distributed far and wide in the garden, in and out of containers and the ground. This is the thriftiest grass there is. Take a small slice of it and it will not take long to grow into a good size plant.

The other plants I've become enamoured of are alpines — the plants that grow in difficult circumstances and climates and have proven to be incredibly hardy.

Kate Seaver has a business (Kate's Garden) that combines garden maintenance and design with clutterbusting. She knows whereof she speaks when she talks about how to downsize the garden, since she recently moved from a very large house and garden into a smaller version of both. Increasingly, more of her professional design work is about answering the question: How can I simplify my garden and keep its beauty?

Kate puts her clients through their paces. They must know what they need and want before proceeding. Here's what Kate suggests thinking about before you start downsizing your garden:

- How will you use the garden?
- What's the focus? What are the key views? Envision what you really want.
- Where do you sit? What do you see? Create eye candy for yourself.
- Make choices about simplifying your planting. Do you want a garden that's always in bloom? Can you choose colourful, textural foliage instead?
- Make sure any flowering plants you do choose have longer bloom times. Pick plants that are more drought resistant, and don't need staking. (This latter point is extremely important for dahlia lovers — you may have to switch to other beauties.)
- Choose hardy, long-blooming plants such as carpet roses and hydrangeas (the right choice will ensure year-round interest), and long-lived repeat bloomers such as hardy geraniums and salvia — when you cut them back, they will return for another display.
- Simplify the colour scheme.
- Use stalwart plants, not ones that give you a headache.
- Choose carefully: At this stage, you do not want to make mistakes that must be fixed two years down the road.

Fear of change can work against you in gardening. Think in longer sweeps of time, and you'll have created a vision not only for your garden but also for your life.

Downsizing in Stages

Once you've decided to downsize the garden, the first step in the process is to sort out how much space to do without. The idea is to bring the essential garden closer to the house to make it more accessible. You can do this easily by adding interior fences and screens. Here are a few suggestions:

+ Make a courtyard inside the garden. Sort out how much space you can sensibly garden and build a fence around it.
+ Outside this designated area, make a forest, a meadow, or a natural wild area. Wild areas, however, still require attention, so don't think you can abandon that part of the garden. Wild and weedy is not the aim; the goal is to extend the natural ecology of the garden by using combinations of native plants.
+ Turn more and more of your garden into clusters of evergreens. They require almost no maintenance, must be watered less often than deciduous plants, and once mulched, can be left alone. Combine them with some ornamental grasses and you have a happy combination of static forms and perpetual movement.
+ Divide up the garden into specific "rooms" that you can

change one at a time. The farther away a room is from the house, the more likely it will change radically to become self-sufficient.

- Move all the working elements of the garden, such as a composter or a potting bench, close to the house. You don't want to have to schlep too far on one hand, but on the other you don't want to give up good habits.

- Before you even think about doing a downsizing renovation, make sure you know where you'll be putting any soil you dig up or any stones you can't use. If they will have to be hauled away, figure out where and when and how much it is likely to cost.

- Hire a qualified arborist to clean out trees and shrubs that have grown unruly over the years. This is a great haircut to start with. It will give you a much better idea of what you've got to deal with.

- Trash any crappy-looking shrubs and don't get sentimental about a big old forsythia or honeysuckle just because your parents had one. If a shrub looks terrible, either get rid of it or have it coppiced (cut right back to the ground to start over again).

- Clean out all the grass and weeds growing in, around, and through plants. My usual procedure is to dig everything up, pull them apart into separate plants, and store them in pots for reuse or re-placement.

When the time comes and I can't get around my garden with ease, I'd seriously consider redesigning many parts of it. I'd use raised beds and install them one section at a time. Kneeling gets worse the older you get (it's the getting-up part that hurts) and I like the look of raised beds.

Always choose a style that's going to work with both your capabilities and the existing style of your garden. If you can't reach very far, make borders shallower (while still allowing as much stretch as possible). Most of us can reach from 2 to 2.5 feet (60 to 75 cm) so the maximum width of the bed would be 4 to 5 feet (1.2 to 1.5 m) if it is gardened from both sides. Having a little path all around a raised bed is going to make it accessible and create an interesting look. If you are wheelchair-bound, then all paths must have a firm, even surface to accommodate that.

I'm mad keen about containers so I'd certainly collect more of them. And I'd invest in only those impervious to winter. There are new containers astounding in their ability to withstand our winter freeze-thaw changes.

Re-vision what the garden will be doing for you. If you have to change your habits and your mind about how much you want to do or can do, then make good plans and work out a timetable so things don't get too difficult and discouraging. *Tempus fugit* all right and a lot faster the older you get.

Downsizing Your Garden Shed

Many years ago, I got discouraged by the amount of garden stuff stacked up in my storage shed. I couldn't see past the mess, but Kate Seaver, ace clutterbuster, could see past it all. She and I recently tackled twenty-odd years of junk I'd accumulated. First, we removed everything from the shed. Then we placed everything into piles:

- **Pile One:** Automatic throw-outs. Anything strange-smelling or falling apart were my benchmarks — straight to the garbage.
- **Pile Two:** Stuff that could be recycled. Reluctantly I put out the stuff I'd bought for grandchildren who will never use them again (sob). Little kids grabbed them up before I could get everything to the curb.
- **Pile Three:** Any foolish items I'd picked up on a whim, or were given to me as a gift. You know, the "cute" things for the garden like herb signs.
- **Pile Four:** Storing like with like. This should be a no-brainer but I found secateurs all over the place. Fourteen pairs of them, and they huddled together finally waiting for their container moment.
- **Pile Five:** Containers. I love collecting containers, bins, and boxes of every ilk. I'm constantly on the hunt for more. What I learned from looking at this pile: Use what's on hand, measure what you'll need in the future, *then* shop. I cannot

tell you how much money this saved me. I still use the same containers we chose then and each still contains the same designated tools.

We put useful items, such as pot shards used for drainage, in one big pot. The big necessary tools, such as spades, were hung on individual nails on the shed door. Best of all was dealing with the organic matter. I had squirrelled away all sorts of bags with a little bit of soil in them, as well as leftover potting material, and fertilizer experiments. All of it was dumped into the composter.

Every year I get rid of something, and it becomes easier and easier to see what to do without. I'm devoted to a very few tools and all the others are stored for future use or gifts — you never know when they'll come in handy. Every item to do with a specific chore — for instance, all the sculpture-fountain doodads; the touch-up paint and sandpaper for fixing up furniture; mending materials; stakes; and so on — was put in an individual container.

It was a really superb exercise in how to make myself more disciplined. I find I don't need to buy as many things as I used to because I know very well what I've got on hand.

SELLING A GARDEN

A handsome house with a terrific garden has great curb appeal. Though you can't put a percentage value on the house, a lovely garden can draw people toward it. Odds are, however, you'll be selling the house

NO REGRETS

Aldona Satterthwaite, executive director of the Toronto Botanical Garden, found that detailed planning is important when downsizing. But even good plans don't always work out quite as expected, and you have to be willing to adapt. Here's her story.

I had it all figured out, or so I thought. My previous house move had taken place in the dead of winter and in the throes of a divorce, and neither my state of mind nor the weather had been conducive to taking divisions from the garden I'd lovingly built up.

This time I was determined that things would be different. Fifteen years had gone by and I was downsizing, leaving behind a lush shade garden stuffed full of plants, many of which would be all the better for being thinned out and divided. Not to mention saving me money.

I'd sold my house at the start of winter, but the closing date wasn't until late May. I reckoned that gave me plenty of time to find another property and pot up some of my prized babies. Yet after trudging through what felt like hundreds of lacklustre houses, I was losing hope. It was spring and homelessness loomed large.

Out of the blue, my dream home came on the market — an old, one-and-a-half-storey farmhouse with a wraparound porch at the edge of a park. While the house and its setting were perfect, the closing date was not. A gap of several months meant putting my things into storage and camping out with assorted family and friends. I knew that hauling around delicate potted plants in the heat of summer was out of the question.

Since that move, I've heard that changes have been made to my old garden to better accommodate life with a toddler. But despite taking not one single plant, I have no regrets. You see, my new garden is wide and sunny and generously dotted with perennials the previous owner left behind — she's moved into a condo. I'm getting reacquainted with roses, and lavender and many other sun-lovers I simply couldn't grow before. In short, I've swapped one much-loved and well-tended garden for another. How's *that* for a bargain?

to someone who, as in my friend Gemma Norton's case, says, "I love the garden," and then proceeds to be baffled by it. Alas, no one loves your garden but you. This leaves a conundrum: What do you do with the garden when you have to move?

Imagine all those wonderful plants you so lovingly acquired going to wrack and ruin, becoming weed-infested or choked out? It is to weep and though it's complicated enough selling a house, this is not the time to ignore selling the garden along with it. If you are moving from an older house with a mature garden, you can bet there will be a renovation and construction and it will be done by people who have no feeling for plants whatsoever, so try doing some of the following things:

♦ Make a list of the mature (but easily moved) plants you could use for your new home. Garden-grown healthy plants are bigger and tougher than most plants found in a nursery. And you know what efforts have been put into them. Make an exclusion of these plants in your listing.

♦ Don't touch plants that are very old and very large. They won't necessarily survive the move. And I wouldn't waste a huge amount of effort on taking perennials, unless you have a serious emotional attachment to them or are convinced you'll never find them again.

♦ Never remove plants once you've signed an agreement — they become the property of the new owners, who don't have to tell you what their plans are even if it's to destroy the entire garden.

♦ If the new owner does indicate that there are going to be major renovations, ask if it's okay to come back and remove some of the intruding plants, especially those close to the house. Promise to take them away for free.

♦ If you see that construction workers are trampling over plants at your old place, offer to go in and get them out of the way.

One complaint I've heard over and over again is that the more complicated a garden, the more terrifying it is for the new owners and the more likely it is they'll be thrown off the sale. Most purchasers will find the garden of a true believer way too hard to look after. My own would certainly be scary and would never be cared for as scrupulously as I care for it. I know every square inch of it and no one else can be expected to have the patience to acquire all that information in a few months when I've had decades.

Make yourself cognizant of who would be attracted to the house. If it's young families, those fabulous complex borders of yours are only going to be an impediment. The simpler and less fussy the garden, the more likely you will be able to sell the house. My garden would be viewed as way too difficult to handle because of its complexity, which is why I'd do the following when we make our final move:

♦ I'll leave all the major hardscaping intact. It's way too expensive to remove, and it looks terrific. Who wouldn't want it? It gives the garden needed shape and even if a buyer hated it, the work would be there as an inspiration.

- I will leave all the major structural plants behind. The magnificent central focus, an old Japanese maple, would be a crime to remove (and a replacement for a plant of this age and distinction would be over $6,000). But I'll take all the smaller, more recently planted goodies around it.

- I would consider putting in a lawn. I almost choke when I write this because I've spent my life taking out lawn areas to make space for more trees and shrubs. But our house would be a magnet for a family and they wouldn't want all those layers and layers of plants. They'd want some place to play ball or run around.

- I'd remove the rare and unusual plants, and either give them away, take them with me, or have a giant sale.

- I'd budget how much it would cost to make the garden simpler and more buyer-friendly — once again, here's where a plant sale would come in handy. Then I would hire someone else to do it. I'm not sure I could bear ripping this place apart myself.

- I would remove the sculpture-fountain because artist Reinhard Reitzenstein promised, "When you move, we'll work out a system to get it out of here." It weighs about two tons (1.8 metric tons) and it has become a very important part of my life. But if I moved to an apartment and couldn't take it with me, I'd exclude it from the sale of the house and sell it separately or donate it to a gallery or museum.

TRUE REAL ESTATE ADVICE

I have been taking designing and gardening advice from my old friend Ted Johnston for decades so when he became a real estate agent, I took his thoughts very seriously. He sells both city and cottage country properties, with the following cautions:

When I value a house, I add on a price for the garden, just as I would for high-end appliances, a fireplace, that sort of thing. I am fortunate to know what most gardens are worth so it's easy. But the key point is the garden carries value, like a single or two-car garage, finished versus unfinished basement.

A house with a nice entrance garden is going to give potential buyers a good feeling before they even enter the house. In older homes, foundation plantings, for example, usually block the front door — a clear message "don't come in here" — or they block light from getting into dark basements. My favourite quote (and I have no idea where I read this): "Foundation plantings make a trailer look like a home and a home look like a trailer."

So the garden is another tool to sell the house: It sets the curb appeal, it sets the immediate impression of the house. It's very important and quite often I will do the garden or have it done before I list a house — I know because many of the gardens I've created have sold the house. I once sold a house and had the garden materials excluded from an offer; it was a negotiating tool and it worked.

The need to have really good advice on how to market your garden is absolutely paramount. But here's a thought for a new service business: "A Holding Station," where a team of experts comes in, digs up the plants, cares for them while the owner moves or renovates, and then delivers them to the new garden and plants them. Any experienced gardener is going to want the garden around the new house to be started as quickly as possible, so it's always wise to check out your local garden centre and see if they will take a few of your big plants (indoors or out) for safekeeping for a price. You never know. So don't even think about leaving your whole garden behind. Find friends who might have some space for storing your most precious plants. If you don't, you'll end up regretting the loss. Although you can't take your garden with you, you can take some of the signature plants to put in another garden or even a container. Memories are made of the plants we love best.

Fluffing the Garden for Sale

You may be fortunate enough to have an agent who actually knows how to make a garden more appealing when it's up for sale. On the other hand, you can spend a fortune having a professional fluffer or stager improve the garden. The following, however, are some easy thrifty tips to make your house look absolutely perfect from the outside and give it the curb appeal that will draw people inside:

- This is *the* most important thing to do: **Make sure you've weeded every area in the yard.** When someone's looking for a new house, neglect outside signals neglect inside.
- Remove all the clutter, absolutely every little bit of muck you

can see from the street. Do this on a daily basis, in case bits
and pieces fly in overnight.

♦ Edge the sidewalks, pathways, and borders so they are pin
neat.

♦ Dress up the lawn: Leave no empty spots — consider re-
seeding if the lawn looks torn up by animals. Buy a small bit
of sod, cut it into pieces, push it into place, and water deeply.
Add a layer of compost as well.

♦ If you have gaps in any of the borders, tuck in some bright,
harmonizing annuals.

♦ If the driveway and walk look battered, get them repaired.
This isn't expensive and will automatically make the house
look refreshed.

♦ Power-wash everything in sight. You can rent these machines
cheaply. Go over the porch, walkways, and driveway.

♦ Make sure there's no debris floating about the swimming
pool, and there are pleasant plantings (even if you have to
resort to containers) around the exterior.

♦ Fix broken lights.

♦ Make sure windows sparkle.

♦ If you've got a huge suburban front lawn, add a small group of
trees, shrubs, and ornamental grasses to make it stand apart
from all the other houses in the neighbourhood. It will also
give the front of the house a little protection from the road.

♦ Make sure there are no gloomy overgrown foundation plants

blocking the light to the interior. Old evergreens respond well to being whacked back, but get it done by someone who knows what they are doing.

♦ Do something simple and daring: Install or move one great plant, one that makes everyone stop dead, and put it in an obvious spot.

♦ The *coup de grâce*: Put welcoming planted containers on either side of the entrance, maybe a pair at streetside near the path if you have one, and definitely a pair flanking the front door. This is a small investment and you can always take the plants with you when you move. If you run out of time, have a garden consultant get some good-looking containers and fill them. It's money well spent and you won't lose anything on it.

Fluffing a garden for sale can be one of the most sensible, and thriftiest, things you can do when selling the house. It will welcome people into your life, make them like what you've created around you, and maybe persuade them that this is the best place in the world to live.

CREATING A NEW GARDEN IN A NEW SPACE

It's not the easiest thing to do — creating a new garden. It's best to get started in a small way just by dealing with what's immediately around you. Don't try to do everything at once. It's important to be in a house for at least two seasons, preferably three, to see what's there. But you can get a start with the following thrifty tips:

- Don't try to replicate your old garden. This is folly. You've got a new space, a new environment, and possibly new climate zones, so clear your mind and try something altogether new.
- If you must take a few of your plants with you and have excluded them from your sale, co-ordinate their removal with the new owner of your old property. If your move is in winter, mark the plants you can't live without.
- Learn your space: Again the light, the wind, the rain shadow are all-important factors in a new garden.
- Pick new plants that work with the scale of the new garden. Don't have any ambitions for huge plants to start with. Best to let plants grow into their own space.
- Try to organize some form of uprights (plants or screens) to give a sense of privacy and create an outdoor wall.
- If the new garden feels cramped, scrounge mirrors from the recycling or garbage. It's astounding how many of these are tossed. Put them on a fence, angled, flat, behind plants, and they will expand a very small space.

By not remaking your old garden, you are a step ahead of the game. You can look at things with new eyes and make a fresh start on what could be one of the best adventures of your life.

Moving, changing your life around, can be about as stressful as a divorce or a death in the family. You have to be very careful about how many demands you put upon yourself and how much you expect in the future. The garden can be an enormous help in selling a house, but it can also be used as a transition from one stage of your life to another. It can help you fulfill the longing to be creative, to have a contact with nature, and to make that all-important step to being a steward of the environment.

CHAPTER TEN

THE TOP 20 THRIFTY GARDENING TIPS

Here are some of my favourite suggestions from this book, ones that will keep you in good shape and will make gardening so much easier. Never let the garden become a burden. So many people falter when they realize that there is no such thing as a no-work garden. You can have low maintenance, but it is relative. Low maintenance means you have lots of trees, shrubs, and ground covers, and usually it means you are hiring someone else to do it.

A thrifty gardener to my mind is someone quite special — someone who makes very considered judgments before committing themselves to any action, someone who isn't guided just by money, but by how well the money is being used. These suggestions will help you become a thrifty gardener:

1. Start small. Be a patient gardener and you will be a frugal gardener. Buy small shrubs and trees, and let them grow into their space. You will get to know them, and they will adjust to your garden and do a magnificent job of gracing it.

2. Use as many recycled containers, materials, and everyday items as you can. You don't have to buy hugely expensive things if you use your imagination.

3. Save seeds from the food you eat and learn how to grow your own. You can even regrow leeks, cabbages and cilantro. Put the roots back into the soil and water regularly.

4. Learn to propagate plants. This is the thriftiest of all garden strategies. If you join a plant society, they will have a seed exchange; seed catalogues will give you a huge amount of information. To ensure success, buy seeds and seedlings that are local to your region.

5. Learn to divide plants as quickly as you possibly can. This is important especially if you have a lot of space to fill up. If the weather is favourable, you can divide all through three seasons.

6. Before you start to garden, appraise what you have already. Can it be fixed? Would moving a few plants around make it a much prettier place? Or does the garden need a complete renovation?

7. If you decide to renovate the garden, make sure you know what your budget is and how much you would like to spend each year — don't try to do it all at once.

8. Be sure to have a design in your head, on paper, or even on some sticky notes in magazines. Know where you are going.

9. Compost somehow, somewhere on your property, even if it's just a hole in the ground or a plastic bag on the balcony.

10. Mulch with a mix of composted pine bark and compost. Experiment with other forms of mulch such as pebbles, gravel, or shells.

11. Never ever throw out leaves unless they are seriously diseased. Collect them from other people. Use them in the composter, rake them up on top of borders where they will be broken down by worms.

12. Make sure you mulch in spring before things get too big — it's easier to spread the mulch around. Then mulch again after the hard frost hits in the autumn.

13. Never overtidy the garden. Don't cut down all the perennials; leave seeds for the birds, and standing stems to catch the snow or make winter shadows.

14. If you are having a problem with your garden, or feel you can't "see" it properly, hire an expert. Sometimes a pair of fresh eyes on an old problem can give you a very creative solution.

15. Consider a part of your garden budget for ongoing maintenance. Without good care, a garden can revert to nature's whim in a couple of years.

16. Learn to water your garden properly. This is one of the major tasks a garden presents. The water must go deep enough into the soil for it to get below the roots and encourage deep root growth. Work out a system that will not be a huge burden. Make a plan for when you have to be away for more than a few days.

17. Never go by a junkyard, second-hand store, or garage sale without seeing if there's a treasure that could be used in your own garden.

18. Have a yard sale of your own. Don't save up all those garden tools; keep lean and mean and make a little money. Then if you need something new, you've got the cash.

19. Research your plants to make sure that you are putting the right plant in the right place. Co-habiting plants will need the same light, amount of water, and type of soil, which means you have to know what kind you have in your own garden.

20. Study, research, look at pictures, and become visually articulate. Have a vision of what you want, what you need, and then scale it to what you can do.

Gardening has been the major focus of my life for almost forty years. I've puttered, I've gone at it with ferocious intensity at some periods of my life. I've tried most of the tips you'll find in this and the other books I've written, but mostly I like whatever it is I'm doing at the moment. That would be the plants I'm currently most fascinated by. I love to learn about them: about how they grow, where they came from, and what I can put them with to enhance the beauty of the other plants around.

My garden is full of secret nooks that will have a plant put in really the wrong spot: you know, the smaller plant behind bigger ones. We all do it and sometimes I do it deliberately so that in some future season I'll surprise myself — aha, I say, scrabbling around, here's something new and interesting.

But then, for me, everything in gardening is new and exciting. I have never ever lost the sense of pleasure I get when I gaze at the garden backlit with early morning sunshine. It seems the most extraordinary, amazing, marvellous place on earth. I never forget how lucky I am to have a garden.

ACKNOWLEDGEMENTS

This book, like all other books, is a co-operative venture. But this book, unlike a lot of other books, came about over a promotional lunch. I was doing an authors' book brunch promoting *Thrifty: Living the Frugal Life with Style*. Sarah MacLachlan, president and publisher of House of Anansi Press, had lugged me there, thus mucking up her own weekend and being the kind person she is by being supportive. After I finished doing my number, she leaned over and whispered, "Want to do a book called *Thrifty Gardening?*" *Oh yes, please,* was the instant response. Within a day, the wonderful Janie Yoon, my editor on the *Thrifty*, was in touch and we went off to hammer out an outline. The speed of all of this is so rare in the usual gavotte of the publishing world, that it astounded me then and still does now. Much thanks to the inimitable Karen York, who copyedited this book.

When I first starting writing gardening books back in the 1980s, the only things you could consult, besides gardeners, were books and magazines. Nowadays, there are fewer of the latter but more people gardening. The Internet has some absolutely glorious web sites that flourish amid all the noise and dreck of the World Wide Web. And e-mail, which none of us could survive without now (or so we think), has become a useful garden writer's tool. I put out the call to the gardeners who subscribe to my newsletter, the designers, the friends, the nursery owners for tips and suggestions, and to share what they are doing in their gardens now. I cannot express how grateful I am to them. I learn new stuff every day, which is why it's so hard to write a book. Many, many of their ideas have been incorporated here; some we just didn't have room for and I apologize. But we've selected the best, and believe me these people are the best at whatever they are doing.

- Tony Avant, whose superb web site, www.plantdelights.com, has lots of pix and info
- Donna Balzer, co-author with Steven Biggs of *No Guff Vegetable Gardening*
- Margot Belanger, gardener
- Ann Boyd, gardener
- Box Design, landscape architects, www.boxdesign.com
- Dugald Cameron, who has a great catalogue with tons of information, www.gardenimport.com
- Philippa Campsie & Norman Ball, www.parisianfields.com
- Denise Carr, gardener
- Karen Chapman, container designer, www.lejardinetdesigns.com
- Adrienne Clarkson, gardener and author of *Room for All of Us*

- Carole Cowan, director of Zebra Productions and balcony gardener
- Yvonne Cunnington, www.countrygardener.blogspot.com
- Larry Davidson has a superb web site, the best for accurate information on plants: www.losthorizons.ca
- Sonia Day, author of *The Untamed Garden, Incredible Edibles*, and *The Urban Gardener*, www.soniaday.com.
- Mark Disero, is proprietor of www.gardentoronto.ca, www.gardentoronto.ca
- Susan Dyer, gardener, partner in children's store Advice from a Caterpillar, www.advicefromacaterpillar.ca
- Heidi Ehlers, gardener
- Rob Firing, Director of Publicity and Communications at HarperCollins Canada and gardener
- Sander Freedman, principal of Sander Design, www.sanderdesign.ca
- Kelly Gilliam, www.theseedbank.net
- Esther Giroux, garden maker and great friend
- Gil Goldstein, real estate agent
- Kees Govers, www.liveroof.ca
- William Grainger, biology teacher and host of *Growing with Grainger*
- Doug Green, garden blogger and author, www.simplegifts-farm.com
- Susan Harriell, gardener

- Eulice Harris, gardener
- Fereshteh Hashemi, gardener and historian
- Uli Haverman, gardener and horticulturist at Plant World
- Dan Heims, Terra Nova Nurseries, www.terrranova.com
- Dan Hinkley, botanist, plant collector, and author of three books, www.danielhinkley.com
- Tom Hobbs, author of *The Jewel Box Garden*, www.southland-snursery.com
- Rebecca Horwood, gardener and financial consultant
- Grace and Roger Inglis, gardeners
- Dan Jason, www.saltspringseeds.com
- Ted Johnston, gardener, life coach, and real estate agent
- Michele Landsberg, gardener and author of *Battle Axioms: Second Wave-First Hand*
- Andrew Lawson, author of *Imaginary Gardens*
- Joerg Leiss, propagator and member of the Ontario Rock Garden & Hardy Plant Society
- Blaine Marchand, gardener
- Cheryl Moss, www.ponderingsfromthepond.blogspot.com
- Lara Lucretia Mrosovsky, author of *An Illustrated Guide to Growing Food on your Balcony* in collaboration with Green Thumbs Growing Kids, The Hincks-Dellcrest Centre
- Colette Murphy, www.uharvest.ca
- Valerie Murray, ace gardener and friend
- Gemma Norton, garden designer

- Nick Palumbo, garden designer
- Barry Parker, extraordinary city gardener and seed collector
- Sherry Patterson, member of Community Served Agriculture and proprietor of Chick-a-Biddy Farms
- Sandra Pella, Head Gardener of Toronto Botanical Garden
- Barry Porteous, gardener in the country
- Liz Primeau, gardener and author of *The Front Garden* and *Growing Garlic*
- Lorraine Robertson, gardener
- Malka Rosenberg, balcony gardener
- Aldona Satterthwaite, Executive Director of Toronto Botanical Gardens, www.torontobotanicalgarden.com
- Kate Seaver, Kate's Garden, www.katesgarden.com
- Louise Sleman, gardener
- Deborah Smith, gardener by the sea
- Mary Vinci, owner of Studio 990 and terrace gardener
- Bev Wagar, Seedy Saturday in the Vienna Café, Port Burwell, Ontario
- Edward O. Wilson, author of *The Social Conquest of Earth* and *The Diversity of Life*.
- Tim Wood, Spring Meadow Nursery, www.springmeadow.com
- Karyn Wright, Terra Edibles, www.terraedibles.com
- Harvey Wrightman, Wrightman Alpine Gardens, www.wright-manalpines.com — he has the best videos of any nursery: funny and articulate. Incredible plants.

♦ Karen York, garden writer, author of *The Holistic Garden*, invaluable friend and the invaluable copyeditor of this book.

GARDEN SOCIETIES:

I belong to the Toronto Botanical Garden and find that belonging to a botanical society keeps me in touch with the garden community, plant sales, and superb talks from knowledgeable people.

I'm also a member of the Ontario Rock Garden & Hardy Plant Society, www.onrockgarden.com.

PRODUCTS SOURCES:

Check out www.rittenhouse.ca. It's a catalogue house with great products, superb service, and I write their newsletter, which is a lot of fun. Lee Valley has Bag Balm along with tons of other garden stuff, www.leevalley.com.

FOR HERITAGE SEEDS:

Check out www.saltspringseeds.com, www.annapolisseeds.com, www.terraedibles.ca, Urban Harvest at www.uharvest.ca, www.seeds.ca. Seeds of Diversity is a great place to source seeds, www.seedsofdiversity.com.

ABOUT THE AUTHOR

MARJORIE HARRIS is considered the country's best-known gardener. She is the national gardening columnist for the *Globe and Mail* and has written several bestselling gardening books, including *Ecological Gardening* and *How to Make a Garden*. She has also written *Thrifty: Living the Frugal Life with Style*, an inspiring and practical guide to living the frugal but fulfilling life. She lives in Toronto with her husband, the writer Jack Batten.